BRAVE VOICE

An Invitation
to Speak,
Listen,
and Love
from the Heart

HEATHER BICKEL STEVENSON

BRAVE VOICE

An Invitation
to Speak,
Listen,
and Love
from the Heart

HEATHER BICKEL STEVENSON

Story
Sanctum
PUBLISHING

To mi amor, Jer… the one who drew out my voice, has championed it, and never sought to silence me. This is for you!

TABLE OF CONTENTS

PROLOGUE

BEFORE I GET INTO SHARING the intimate details of my story, the deep struggles and amazing joys, I want to start by saying I am thriving, loving life again, and more healthy than I have been in years, but still not fully well physically. I have been so thankful to walk through much of what you are about to read together with my dear husband Jer for the last 11-plus years! He has been my rock, my best friend, my biggest cheerleader–the one who has truly seen me at my absolute worst and loved me unconditionally through it. It was hard to wait until I was 36 to find "the one" and get married, but it was totally worth the wait.

The following pages will take you through many stories of my life that have never been told before except to some family and my super close girl friends. It's a true story of my darkest days, hardest moments, deepest joys, and how I got through all of it to bring me to where I am today. It's an honest story of despair and hope, light and darkness, faith and fear. It's a story of how the faithfulness of God was steadfast even when I felt I had very little faith. I am an ongoing work in progress; aren't we all? Through all of these stories, my "true voice" was being formed and now I have a passion to help others find theirs! I hope you can find yourself somewhere in these pages and find your unique voice that you can contribute for the good of this world.

INTRODUCTION

I BEGAN THINKING OF WRITING A BOOK during the middle of the pandemic. It was during a time when I was not sure if I would be alive much longer because of the following illnesses that I had all at once: I had gotten so sick with postural orthostatic tachycardia syndrome (POTS), chronic fatigue, mold toxicity, small fiber neuropathy, irritable bowel syndrome (IBS), outlet dysfunction, ongoing severe insomnia, post concussive syndrome, Lyme disease, and so much more. I began to not be able to get out of bed because of how weak I was. It was quite the timing as it was when the world had shut down with the pandemic. I felt helpless. I wanted to help so many others, yet I found myself needing so much help. It was hard to ask for help from my local community since everyone was understandably themselves in such survival mode. My world became oh-so small. No longer could I show up and provide counseling, soul companioning, coaching, nursing, growing my business, or being there as a listening ear for whoever needed one. It all came to a screeching halt.

I could no longer numb the dark and hurting places in my soul by being busy, which it seems I did most of my life. I did not hear from many people as everyone needed to go into their own bubble to survive. I understood, but it still hurt. Without the energy to even go outside, I could not continue finding my significance in being the "neighborhood nurse" or in my performance in any sense. Without having the capacity to maintain correspondence, I could not find my security in being liked or approved of. I found myself bed-bound and weighing under 90 pounds. My days consisted of trying to survive and going to doctor after doctor and enduring the most gruesome of medical testing.

Honestly, there were days when I no longer wanted to live, and almost no one knew it. I just didn't feel I had any purpose in my days. I imagine many others might have gone through a dark night of the soul for one reason or another, and many during the pandemic just like me. The suffering I was enduring to survive each day was so profound. Dealing with upwards of 100 symptoms and barely able to sit up, life felt meaningless.

When I did not know if I was going to live, I started to share a lot more details of my back story with my dear husband Jer, because I thought I better get it all out since I did not know if I would be here to share it. I told him (and a few others) what I would want at my funeral. I began to think a lot about what I would want to leave behind. It probably sounds morbid, but I felt I did not have much time left and there was so much more I wanted to say.

I remember asking God one day, "Is there anything left undone that You want me to do?" and that day I did contact some people and say some things that had been on my heart. I also realized as my vision was getting worse during these illnesses that I might not be able to write anything, and I had not been able to journal much because of the vision issues.

I shared my stories with Jer and with my close friends who are like sisters. The funny thing is that both Jer and I have *terrible* memories. I mean *terrible*! So I thought, if I wanted stories to exist in this world after I am gone, I better start writing, and Jer backed that fully! Jer was the first to say, "Sorry, but I *can't* remember well." I am the same. It makes us a perfect fit. We watch movies over and over and can tell the same stories to each other and always hear them afresh and with new ears because we don't remember hearing the stories before, or at least not all the details. I depended on my avid journaling to write this book.

I knew beyond a shadow of a doubt that it was time to write, but the "why" behind this book goes beyond thinking my days were coming to an end quickly—which they still may be before this is even in print. We never know when our last day is, do we? Many of us have lost people dear to us during the pandemic or before. I write because throughout my life, I have found myself shifting who I am, editing and filtering my own voice to "fit in," to be liked and approved of—whether that be a good girl growing up in the south, a nursing student who was scared to death on the inside/feeling like an imposter, a female counseling student at a very conservative seminary in the North where for the most part I didn't feel welcome as a woman, a confused girlfriend who believed I needed to do and say whatever was expected of me to be accepted by whomever I was dating at the time, a white girl from the suburbs living and working in the inner city in Philly, a very sick (and head-injured) patient who didn't want my identity to be pinned on being sick, a friend and mentor to many with a fear of not being loved if they really knew the true me.

I was a girl, born and raised in Georgia, living in Philly, and then in California. I began to really find myself and my true voice while living in California, but was often afraid to share it with many in my life because I was afraid I would be rejected. Yes, a fear of failure and of rejection has been what has kept me from sharing my story in a raw and open way. I fear disapproval from people in GA thinking "she is way too liberal and gone off the deep end." I fear my California community thinking "look how conservative she is." But it's *so* not about all of that! For me, it's about loving God and loving people right where they are.

As I saw my life flash before my eyes in recent years, I began to think, the time is now to share. I want others, especially women who are stuck like me, afraid of what others will think, to find the freedom to share their stories too without filters and without fear. The biggest reason I have not shared sooner is actually not because of others, it's because of my own inner critic. That voice in my head that says, *Heather, you are a wreck, you have nothing of worth to share. You are just going to upset people. You are not who people think and no one will want to read this. Just stay quiet. Stay small. No one wants to listen. What will people think and how will they respond? DON'T DO IT! What do you really have to say that matters? Who would want to read this?* Blah, Blah, Blah. These were the harsh words that came across my heart as I began to type, editing my own words just as soon as they were written. Yep, this is the filter that I have been controlled by for so long.

How many of you deal with that internal editor or critic? How many of you feel scared or like an imposter and have gone your whole life hearing that internal harsh voice? Is it my voice? Is it the devil's voice? Is it the voice of those who have hurt us or rejected us? Maybe it's all of the above, but I hope that this book will give you more freedom to share your voice, to share your story.

I am convinced there are people who want to know the real and authentic *you*! I am so thankful to have some friends like this, who want to know the real me. I don't want others to go down the same road I have for much of my life: living small, living afraid, wondering if others will love and accept me! You and I are free! In my own vulnerability with this book, I hope to help give you the permission to find a few others and have a space where you can be vulnerable and share the true *you* through finding your own brave voice!

CHAPTER 1

BEFORE I FOUND MY
AUTHENTIC VOICE

LIFE WAS FULL GROWING UP and there were so many gifts that came with growing up in our home. I was involved with girl scouts, clogging, tap, swim team, soccer and gymnastics. We spent holidays with extended family or with friends of our family, fished at the lake, held lemonade stands, went golfing, played spot-light tag, had exchange students or other people that lived with us for short or long periods of time. Some people came from overseas, and others were friends of ours that for one reason or another needed a safe place to stay.

Some of my favorite memories growing up included going to Florida for a week in the summers for a vacation or other fun family trips that my mom planned. It was a time when work was put aside and we could really be together as a family—me, my brother (Brandon), my mom (who goes by Smokey), and my dad (Art). It was the only time my dad was able to be truly present and not travel for work or on the phone for work on the weekends. Mom was so good at planning fun vacations that all of us really enjoyed.

Our favorite trip as a family was rafting the Colorado River at the bottom of the Grand Canyon. Our whole family felt free from other distractions and the four of us just got to be together in nature for seven days rafting. We got to talk with each other and tell stories about years past. We had so much fun, I was so amazed to see the Grand Canyon from the bottom looking up, and we all bonded together in special ways. There were times that we were away from home and out of our normal day-to-day stressors, it was truly a gift, and one that I will never forget.

It was also a gift that my mom was so open to always allow us to have friends over and even have people live with us throughout our growing up years who needed a place to stay. Our home was a lively home, always filled with people and lots going on. I believe this was quite different from what my parents had growing up. My parents are some of the most generous people I have ever known. They will give to literally anyone in need. They will provide whatever they can. They would give the clothes off of their back if someone needed them. These actions spoke loudly and shaped my heart of giving as well. They never held back.

Life was so busy growing up. I sometimes wonder now if this busyness kept me from having to face my true fears or learn to listen to or make use of my own voice? Swim team, family trips, clogging, dance, gymnastics, jazz, ballet, fun birthday parties for myself and friends, baby sitting, band, camps (for church, sailing, and horseback riding), hours of playing in the backyard in the woods, playing in the creek and building forts, friends over to play or spend the night, piano lessons, dinner at church on Wednesday nights, out to dinner several other nights of the week since dad was traveling and we were so busy, and the list goes on.

My Life Even Began With a BANG

I was told by my parents that I came out of the womb ready

to run. My mom had to be rushed to the hospital by a family friend an hour from our home for a C-section to have me. I was a double footling breech (meaning both feet were down, and I was standing straight up). When my mom went into labor, it was over a month early and I was teeny tiny! I can't imagine my dad being prepared to be a dad, having traveled his whole career, nor my mom, who had a very rough upbringing, being prepared to basically be a single mom as dad continued to travel Monday through Friday for work. I was here as their first baby and my brother was born 16 months later. My Dad was on the road when I was born (he is the hardest worker I have ever known!). Even though some trucks got in front of him and behind him to help rush him back to Atlanta, the C-section happened before he could get there.

I am told that I was quite the challenge as a baby and a toddler—not wanting to eat or sleep, walking later than all the other toddlers, and being the last to be potty trained. I always had an upset stomach and cried quite a bit. As a toddler, I was not happy to have a little baby brother around that needed all of the attention. Apparently, I even bit my mom on the leg one day when she was breastfeeding my brother. I guess I learned quickly and at a young age what I thought I needed to do to try to get attention, even though it was quite an unhealthy approach, and it was without using words. *But biting my mom on the leg! Really?*

According to my mom, I was not too excited to interact with people I didn't know. I became very protective of my brother when strangers approached us in the grocery store. I'm not sure if that was from me being shy or maybe just from being overwhelmed.

Once we were in our school-aged years, my brother and I became quite the active duo. We were given so many opportunities and were loved well. Even though he and I were 16 months apart in age and had our spats, he was/is my closest friend for sure. No one else really knew what we knew or experienced life as we did. It was he and I and we stuck together. We spent a ton of time together in the summers especially, when my mom would work, we would do chores and then spend the day at the neighborhood pool. We played a lot and had friends over all of the time. It was a gift to grow up in one small town and be in the same schools as my brother for elementary, middle and high school. All of this was the opposite of what my mom grew up in, as she moved constantly with being from a military family. She wanted us to have it all.

My brother and I played hard outside everyday after school. On the weekends we would listen for my dad's unique whistle, as we knew that was the signal that it was dinner time. Sadly, it seemed there was little time for us to share our thoughts with dad since he was gone during the week and had to work at home on the weekends to prepare for his work the coming week. My mom was busy too, but they both did the absolute best that they could parenting and providing for us.

One special time we had to share a little bit with mom was during what we called "lap time." This is where we would sit on mom's lap and chat or next to her and watch a show. It was a time that we really looked forward to each day, and it was also a time that my brother and I could delay going to bed. Just *"one* more *show"*!?

Looking back, I wish that those times could have been times of sharing how we were really doing and feeling. I don't know that any of us in the family were really in touch with that, or even if we were, I don't think we had the ability, freedom, skills or courage to share it. We did have a few minutes at night one-on-one when mom would "tuck us into bed" and we would say our prayers together. I sure hated going to bed though, and would often either sleepwalk or go and crawl in bed with my mom in my growing up years. I did not like being alone and didn't see the value in being alone.

As a little girl I remember seeking to make sure that my mom and dad were alright, and I took care of my little brother as much as I could when mom would go to work at 6am in the morning before we went to school. I would crawl in bed with him, saying that I wanted to keep him safe, but really it was because I was scared.

I Was Taught It's Not OK to be "Not OK"

In fact, one day someone tried to break into our house early in the morning after my mom went to work, but our poodle barked non-stop until the person ran away from the house through the woods. I honestly was scared from that point forward, even when it came to an age where I was able to babysit others! I tried to hide my fear and true feelings. I made up excuses as to why I could not babysit and only agreed to if my brother went with me. I wonder why I didn't feel the freedom to verbally express this intense fear I felt in these situations.

I learned intuitively while growing up in the south that if anyone asked how I was, my answer was always supposed to be, "fine." And if I asked anyone else how they were, I expected to hear the answer "fine." There was this pressure to appear that I was feeling great, and that is what I wanted others to think. Looking back and even experiencing it as an adult, it can be so maddening! Why (in the South and maybe everywhere else and in life in general) do we have to pretend like we are "just fine?" To put on a happy face, to have a perfectly organized home, and to appear as a family that all is well. I mean, how many of us really are *fine* and have everything together? I know I sure don't have it together... never have.

I won't ever forget the day in elementary school when I got to drive the tractor in the yard, and it was considered "safe" because the blades had been removed. Usually, I would let my brother drive it because he was better at it and it had a little basket on the front where I could sit. One day I decided to give it a try and I drove over some stones in the yard, and it threw my brother in front of the tractor. Me and the tractor ran over my brother. Seeing him in pain and hurt was one of the scariest days of my life. My mom sent me across the street to be watched by the neighbor while she whisked him to the ER. I never got to share the fear, shame, and sorrow for what happened. Thankfully after some stitches and X-rays, he was sent home and not permanently damaged.

Another time I sent him to the ER was when I piled pillows up in the living room and swung him around with his arms and would let go at just the right time so he would land on the pillows. Sadly, some of the pillows were poorly placed by a table and his head hit the table. This ended up with him getting stitches yet again and another trip to the ER. Although these were accidents, I felt so much guilt and felt I had nowhere to express it, beyond crying in my bed at night.

My mom was always responding to medical emergencies in our own home or anytime we saw one while we were out and about. I sure was amazed watching her and wanted to make her happy. I even got to help her sometimes with these emergencies we would see (it's probably what has helped prepare me to this day to respond to emergencies, especially car accidents and almost every time I fly). I *loved* getting to help her or help anyone. This has been true even when I was a little girl. Mom said that the 5-year-olds down the street in our neighborhood would come to me "for counseling or help." I knew what I needed to say to help others, but ironically, I had no idea how to express what I needed, or how to share what I was thinking about.

Early on in elementary school I got to be close friends with another little girl named Amanda. We had the same pj's and identical stuffed animals. We were almost inseparable. I will never forget the day when I found out that my dear friend Amanda had cancer in 4th grade. She was so brave and would tell me not to worry. She would say that she knew God was with her and she was not afraid. Her words were powerful and have stayed with me ever since. She didn't speak much, but when she did, everyone listened, even the adults! I would accompany her to chemo and radiation most weeks in 4th grade. We had a lot of chats while she was having treatment. I knew that we could tell each other anything.

Amanda didn't want me to be sad, as she was not afraid to die. The cancer spread throughout her body quite quickly and when I was sent away for summer camp, she passed. I was so angry that I was not with her when she died. As I sat on the front row of the biggest church I had ever been to that was filled to capacity for her funeral, I will never forget an adult telling me to not cry and that I needed to be strong. Looking back, I can't imagine losing the closest person to me (especially at that age, or any age) and not crying. I still struggle to cry to this day. Through this experience, I internalized that I was not to give voice to my sadness and pain.

The Listening Ears of Extended Family and Friends

I learned a lot from my Grandma Esther (my mom's mom) who would come help my mom each year for several months while my dad was traveling for work. She would sneak into my room at night and promise me some peanut butter bread (my favorite snack) if I would listen to stories about God. She had a huge impact on my heart in helping me understand the heart of God for me. I would often find her shuffling through our house with our poodle following close behind or sitting in the rocker in the guest room writing letters of encouragement to others back in her hometown of Iowa. She was soft spoken, hard of hearing, and had the biggest heart I had ever known. It was hard to believe that she had had such a hard life. She was badly abused and endured a horrific marriage yet had such a tender and giving heart. She would ask me about my heart and seemed to have all of the time in the world to listen. What a gift! It didn't seem that there were many adults who seemed to have all of the time in the world to listen, but Grandma Esther sure did. She would listen, listen, and listen some more.

My brother and I sure tried her patience. We gave her a hard time with her cooking, her driving, and her "creative" projects. Sometimes when she would drive going 25 miles per hour, we would yell from the back seat, "step on it, grandma." Was she ever patient! She seemed to always welcome our voice. What an example of love, peace, grace, and kindness. She is my hero.

I also really appreciated the times I got to be with my paternal grandparents in St. Louis, MO. My dad's brother and his family live there and so we spent every other Christmas with my grandparents (Bick and Wease) and my aunt and uncle and cousins. Many fun memories in the snow there! My dad's sister, Aunt Betty, would come for Christmas too and we would dance together, and she has always been so present and kind. My grandma (we called her Wease) was a kind soul. Wease always wanted to hear whatever I wanted to share, and I had no trouble sharing with her or with anyone one-on-one.

During the week when my mom worked as a nurse, my brother and I would get off of the school bus and go next door for a snack and play time at Ta Ta and Uncle Bill's house. They were not related by blood but that is what we called them, because they were "family" to us. We would be allowed to salt the unsalted peanuts if we would listen to a Bible story. They loved us well. They would sit with us while we had our snack and ask us questions about our day. My brother and I had a special relationship with them. Sometimes we would even go on trips with them or spend the night at their house and they had a special drawer with fun little gifts that we got to pick treats out of. If we were sleepy, we got to nap on a little white cloud-like furry rug they had in their living room. They didn't have children, but they treated us like we were family. What a gift!

Yielding to Voices of Authority

I remember as I was growing up, I somehow believed that my voice was to be heard last. I was taught to seek to listen to God's voice, my parents' voices, church leaders, friends, dad's customers, strangers, then last came listening to what I needed. As a kid, I was so intimidated by any voices of authority. I was so afraid even as a kindergartener to speak up in class. If I was called on by the teacher, I could feel my face getting red, my hands shaking and all I wanted to do was crawl under my desk.

I would do literally anything to not get in trouble at school, at home or anywhere. That meant seeking to obey and to be sure to say "yes ma'am, yes sir," and when I answered the phone at home, I answered "Bickel's residence, Heather speaking," because my dad's customers would call our home. I always wanted my parents, Sunday school teachers, schoolteachers, adults, and parents' friends to approve of me. I would take it super hard if I got in trouble or made anything less than an A+ in school.

At school in 4th grade, I had a little crush on a boy and let him cheat off of my paper for a test. We got caught and got sent to the principal's office. I knew as I was doing it that it was wrong, and while in the principal's office I could not find the words to speak. The boy said that I had just slid my paper where he could see it— that he "didn't really want to cheat, but that I made it so easy." This was untrue. He had asked me before class if he could cheat, and I was too nervous to say no. I feared his rejection even though he had never even noticed me before that!

I dreaded anytime that I would get in trouble with my parents or any other adult. I hated doing things wrong or messing up. I would sometimes even write my mom letters and put them under her door at night, asking for forgiveness if I had done something wrong, promising to "not do it again." I know my mom had drawers full of these letters from me! Whenever I got in trouble, I would continue to use my voice to leave more letters of apology under my mom's door. My voice (especially in middle and high school) would get me in quite a bit of trouble when I would back talk. I did learn that I needed to work out things in my head and not out loud.

Getting sent to my room, grounded, and feeling the disapproval of my mom taught me quickly. We would rarely talk about what happened; I left the letters, and that was the end of it.

Acceptance Through Performance

I tried so hard at swimming, soccer, doing my homework, and doing what I was told without arguing. I was never actually really great at anything I tried, but rather I was quite average at everything. I just kind of wanted to blend in with the crowd. I wanted to be *liked* and accepted. But in reality, I never quite felt like I fit in or truly belonged, especially not with the "cool kids." I tried very hard, yet always thought I fell short and could not be accepted for who I truly was. But I was still good at making friends, especially when interacting one-on-one with other little girls.

I sure never wanted my voice to be heard in front of groups of people. In 5th grade, I ran for Student Council and said over the loudspeakers in school, "remember Pickle and vote for Bickel." I remember shaking as I walked to the principal's office to make the announcement and when I walked back to my classroom, it was like a walk of shame. I was laughed at by the other kids in the hallway. I thought, I will never do this again!

I normally would stay quiet about most things, but then there came this one day. It was field day (lots of mini sports competitions at school) and I was by Amanda's side. She was bald at that point because of Chemotherapy and wore a wig to school. She was weak, but she was right there to cheer me and all of the other kids on in their sports. At one moment outside that day, there was a huge gust of wind, and it blew her wig off. Some of the other kids began to mock her and laugh, and *boy* was I mad. I had never yelled at other kids, but I did that day. I was so upset with them, and they knew it. I remember being so angry and then just crying with her afterwards. Seeing tears run down Amanda's face just felt so unfair. Why did my friend have to go through so much and then get made fun of? The empath in me was growing quickly.

I spent a lot of time in the hospital as a child. If I wasn't at the hospital with Amanda, I was at the hospital with mom. Sometimes, if she got called into work at night, my brother and I would go sleep in a hospital room while she worked. While Amanda was sick, I also ended up with a hospital stay of my own with two stomach ulcers and pneumonia. Not fun. I was in so much pain, but I felt I needed to be stoic. This was nothing compared to Amanda's pain. I was told they would put a feeding tube in if I didn't start to eat (the stomach ulcers made it hard to eat), so I snuck my food into the garbage can. I always wanted to do as I was told (or at least be *seen* as doing so), and I felt my actions were a reflection on my mom who worked at that hospital. I was always preoccupied by what others thought, and it impacted what I said and how I acted daily.

My worth throughout elementary, middle, and high school were found in my friendships and in how I was performing in school with grades (we were given one dollar from our parents for every A we got on our report card). I found myself throughout middle school and even high school being very busy, trying to make the best grades, perform well with band, soccer and clogging, even though I would be so scared every time a performance came. I knew I wanted to do my best and make others proud.

As it turns out, I ran at full-steam-ahead from when I was born until I was 36 years old, which is when I got very sick. I started working at 15 and just didn't know how to slow down very well. I wonder if I was so busy on purpose in order to numb something or not to face the insecurities within me, or was this just the normal life of a kid/young adult? Who knows, but I do know that I did not really know myself or make use of my voice or understand my needs or have any direction with respect to where life was headed.

CHAPTER 2

VOICING NEEDS

I WAS NEVER FULLY AWARE OF MY OWN NEEDS, and when I did feel I had a need, I felt it was selfish to ask for that need to be met. I learned that my own needs should come last. I don't remember being told that, it just seemed the way the adults in my life lived, so that was what I internalized. Often when my mom voiced a need, she was told at times "you are being too much." I was very attuned to the needs/wants/desires of others and sought to meet those if I could. This seemed to be my purpose. I really had a lot of fear from a young age but didn't speak about it. I didn't listen to my body either. I had a lot of pain in my abdomen as a little girl, not knowing my body couldn't process wheat, gluten, or dairy well.

It didn't feel like there was room to speak up about what was wrong, what hurt or what I didn't like. I was even asked by teachers in middle school to give them neck massages while watching movies. I never really learned how to say the word, "NO." Even when there were things I wasn't excited to do like orchestra or marching band, I did it even though I didn't want to, and I don't even think I was aware of the things that I didn't want to do. I just know that I shook like crazy every time I performed at anything. I was so embarrassed by that.

My voice often had the hardest time coming out in authentic ways around any adults or people in authority. There was a fear in me that is hard to explain. I just knew that no matter what, I needed to be respectful. Fear seemed to really stifle my true voice.

I remember during a flute recital that took place in a church that once I had started my piece by myself up on stage, I forgot all of the notes and began to shake. I ran down the middle aisle, only to hide in the bathroom so that I would not be seen. I was always so prepared for any performance, but once I was in front of others, I would go blank. It happened every single time. I would prepare to audition for who would sit in what chair in band class and in performances. The closer you sat to the front of the line, the better musician people knew that you were. I would be ready. Then I would walk into my band teacher's office to audition and go blank. *Ugh.* I hated myself for it. I didn't have anyone to talk to about it and just pretended it didn't happen and moved on.

I was always drawn to people that were on the outskirts. I developed a friendship with a girl that was deaf in high school. I learned sign language to be able to speak with her. One of my best friends was a guy named Keith that a lot of people bullied, and he was treated poorly. I became good friends with him but in my senior year he was killed in a car accident with an 18-wheeler. I will never forget sitting in his parents living room with many other grieving kids and seeing his dear mama weep. Grief was a reality in life, yet one I didn't know how to express or to whom I could express it. It just whirled around inside of my head.

Heading to College

Really throughout my growing up years and as I started

college, I looked for my worth in the opinions of others and in how I was performing. When I went to college this was expressed through me having three jobs on campus, dating the most liked guy who was a junior and known as Mr. Berry (I went to Berry College), and getting involved in every on-campus activity I could. I tried to meet as many students on campus as I could and left notes for all of my new friends in their mailboxes in the student center.

Sadly, before my first week of college, I had a head injury (I got hit in the head and knocked unconscious by a thing called "the human bowling ball"), and this incident had a significant impact on my memory. My grades at the end of the 1st semester at Berry College were a 1.7 GPA. I was put on academic probation.

Serious insomnia had started the night of my head injury, which also had a huge impact on my decision making, which was not so good. With not being able to sleep, this is when some of my chronic (but unseen) health issues began, as it profoundly compromised my immune system. I had such confusion in who I was and what I was going to do with my life. And still, even with the head injury and struggling to relearn how to do all of life, I did not talk much about this. In fact I had made my poor hallmates who knew I had had a head injury promise not to tell the resident assistant on my hall or my parents what had happened.

Turning Points

There were women in my dorm that loved God and they had such joy and love that I knew I wanted. I started to get involved with an on-campus college ministry, and I loved going to those meetings and really hearing people share their stories.

One of those meetings fell on Valentines Day of my freshman year. I had a transforming night on February 14, 1995. I spent the whole night in a chapel on Berry College campus and I told God that night that I was so tired of finding my worth in the opinions of others, in how I was performing, or in what a guy or any other person would say about me. I wanted to find my worth in a way that could not be shaken, to see myself through the eyes of a God that loved me perfectly as I was, because of Jesus.

That night in that chapel on the hill, I sang my heart out in worship songs (songs that hadn't meant anything before that night) until the sun came up. I had no idea what had truly happened, but later learned through my resident assistant, dorm mates and campus ministry friends that *I had come to know Jesus.*

These dear women were so amazing and were so faithful to love me and walk alongside me in my new journey with knowing God. It has been the case since 1995 until now that I have always had someone mentoring me and have mentored others. I do wish that I was taught how to really listen to my own body, soul, thoughts and emotions, to slow down long enough to let the truth really come out and exist with another.

I always felt this pressure whether it be from myself or others, to at least look like I had it together. It was surely *not* the case. In re-reading my piles of journals from college, it was the time that I grew the most spiritually. I grew mainly through being mentored, spending time reading and studying the Bible, attending a great church, going to the 10-week beach projects three times and even a summer trip to Japan with ten other college students. In reading my journals, I see that through those experiences I really grew deep roots in my relationship with God and in knowing who I was as a child of God.

A Wreck on the Inside

The hard part was that I almost immediately started comparing myself to other Christians who seemed to be so diligent in having a quiet time and seemed to "have it together." I sincerely have always felt like a mess on the inside and never have felt like I have had things "together." Philippians 4:6-7 were the first verses that I memorized because I struggled (and continue to struggle) so much with anxiety. Very few people, if any, knew or know that this is the case.

The verses I mentioned say, "Do not be anxious about anything, but in every situation, by prayer and petition, present your requests to God, and the peace of God that transcends all understanding will guard your hearts and your minds in Christ Jesus." Ahh, I just took a deep breath even just writing it out now.

Much of my life has been given to invest in mentoring and walking alongside other women. I could do that literally all day and all night! I have always loved sharing about God's love with anyone that will listen. From being a little girl until now, the deep friendships I have cultivated with women have been a super important part of my life. Also, I think that is how I learned how to really listen to my own voice, as friends and mentors listened deeply to me. I really began to see that my voice mattered in this world.

It was stunning to me that I could also invest in other women and that it made an impact on them. I remember discipling gals in college, and I think I was so much more impacted by them than they were by me. I have had the honor of walking alongside many women as they get married and have kids too, some right after college. I have been a part of countless weddings, though with much fear and social anxiety. I would often shake so hard when in weddings that the petals from my bridesmaid's bouquets would fall to the ground. Talk about embarrassing! Whether it be in mentoring women or in journeying beside brides, my mantra has been that we are accepted by God and pursued by God always. I sure wish I could have fully believed that truth for myself, especially in those moments!

During my sophomore year of college, after not attending the 10-week beach project with campus outreach that all of my other friends had attended between my freshman and sophomore years, I had my first bout of depression. I had spent the summer in Iowa helping my elderly Grandma Esther who I respected so much. Helping on the dairy farm near her house in rural Iowa was amazing, but it meant not connecting with the other students throughout the summer and feeling quite lonely my sophomore year. I have had a few more bouts of depression since then, and never quite knew why nor did I know what to do, how to talk about it or where to get help. It has always felt so hard for me to pursue and receive help. Medication, some counseling and a few close friends have definitely been a grace to me in those times, and the journey in those dark times could be a whole book in and of itself.

Being surrounded by people who loved me growing up and then in college, from the outside I looked like a happy, passionate, secure gal who had it all. On the inside though, I felt like a wreck, had no idea who I was or what I was about and felt no one really knew the true me nor what I was going through. I was surrounded by people, yet often felt lonely and unknown.

These first 18 years of life were a long search in knowing who I was and seeking to find my voice. As you see, there were lots of internal struggles, wondering who I am and what my place was in this world, and wondering if it is safe for my true voice, the *real* messy Heather, to come out and be known. I had real needs but did not yet sense I had permission to express them. I looked outward mostly to find my validation and to know that I was okay, but in the years that followed, I began to look upward and inward to learn how to be authentically who God had created me to be.

CHAPTER 3

LISTENING TO MY OWN
SOUL CRIES

THE GOOD THING ABOUT COLLEGE was that I learned so much about how to listen to the voice of God, and in my opinion, it seems to be the most important voice to listen to. This was before I even knew that I could deeply trust my own inner knowing that was from the Spirit of God living in me. Being mentored by others was always so transformative to me and helped me to listen to that voice.

In college, the main way I learned to listen to the voice of God was through reading and studying the Bible. At that point, in the denomination that I was a part of, I learned that the Spirit of God was mainly speaking through the Bible. I spent countless hours reading and studying the Bible in depth, both on my own and with other women. I also memorized as much of the Bible as I could because I was taught that it would bring life to my Spirit and would be used to draw me to God and help me love others. This was done a lot intellectually, both as a new Christian and in seminary.

Later, when I learned more about spiritual formation and spiritual direction, I began to experience the word of God in a whole new way by engaging the word through an ancient spiritual practice called Lectio Divina. For those who may not be familiar with this practice, it consists of six parts:

1) **Preparation** (silencio): Taking a moment to come fully into the present.

2) **Read** (lectio): Listening for the word or phrase that seems applicable to me.

3) **Reflect** (meditatio): How is my life touched by this word?

4) **Respond** (oratio): What is my response to God based on what I have read and encountered?

5) **Rest** (contemplatio): Rest in the word of God.

6) **Resolve** (incarnation): Incarnate (live out) the word of God.

This is explained more in depth within Ruth Haley Barton's book called *Sacred Rhythms* (p 60-61). This method of learning scripture, which is in a more experiential way, transformed my heart and relationship with God completely! It was no longer just an intellectual exercise.

This has truly caused the word of God to come alive in my heart and have an impact on me as I walk throughout the day. The other form of in-depth study still always has a place, and I am so thankful for memorizing verses like Philippians 4:6-7 and others that have been anchors for my soul that I have come back to over and over. Acts 20:24 is my life verse which grounds me when I am wondering what direction I am going in. This verse says "However, I consider my life worth nothing to me, if only I may complete the task the Lord Jesus has given to me—the task of testifying to God's grace." (Side note: Due to this verse, over the last three years, especially during times when I was bed-bound and discouraged, my sweet number-loving husband tried to encourage me by looking farther ahead and predicting ahead that the year 2024 would somehow be a good, significant year for me. Well, I guess time will soon tell!)

There are many ways to engage God's word, but I have found much freedom in not having a rule (or a "have to" or "ought to") around it. In college, through being involved with campus ministry, I thought I needed to have an hour-long "quiet time,"—a time in the morning when I sat and studied the word and prayed. I felt guilty when I did not have that time. Now, I realize since I don't sleep much (because of the ongoing severe insomnia), I don't like doing this in the mornings. I love reading and reflecting throughout the day and it feels so much freer and my heart engages more fully instead of just my mind. It's been life changing.

I also sought to hear the voice of God through worship, prayer, and very rarely, in times of being still. Those times of stillness were almost non-existent in the beginning of my journey of faith. I heard the voice of God through the wisdom of others, as well. Sometimes I found it hard to personally trust that I was hearing the voice of God to my own heart.

The Voice of a Critic

It seems my own inner voice was most often the voice of a critic. I read in countless pages of my journal what I call the "inner dictator." Can you relate to the reality that I am much harder and more critical of myself than anyone else is? This has been a constant struggle. That voice, the inner critic or harsh dictator inside of me, has stolen so much joy and caused me to doubt myself on a very regular basis. This dictator says if you can't perform well and get your "to do" list done then you are a failure. If people are upset at you, you deserve it and it's your fault. This is not the voice of God.

It is and was so hard to believe that this tender heart of God was pursuing me with a still small quiet voice of love. Always. I still thought I had to earn that love or deserve it some way. It's something I wrestle with to this day. It's not earned. This love is a pure and undeserved gift and it's unwavering, no matter my performance or what others think. I have learned that if I go slower and listen carefully to even my body, if there is any sort of dis-ease, to stop and attend to it quickly. This has led to much more freedom and peace in my heart and a joy that is unshakable. It also quiets the inner dictator and allows me to hear the quiet and tender voice of love when my soul is quieted within me. I love listening, loving, lingering and laughing with others—offering a warm presence where people can be authentic and honest about their journeys.

Something I did learn early on about the voice of God and how God saw me was about my "position in Christ." This (along with thinking often on the unwavering grace of God towards me) is something that radically impacted my faith as a new Christian, and it continues to ground me. It's also something that I have sought to share with every close friend, every person I have mentored, and frankly anyone who will listen. It must be something I need to be reminded of often. This is the reality that I am loved more perfectly than I could ever imagine by God, and nothing can change that. That because of Christ, I am loved, accepted, forgiven, complete, whole, delighted in and rejoiced over. Nothing I do, or don't do, can change this reality! Oh, if I could only believe these truths unwaveringly and really walk in light of them! I have sought to believe this from my freshman year of college and forward!

The World's Greatest Need

I went to the 10-week beach project after my sophomore year and was so clueless as I headed for the training that summer about what I wanted to pursue in college. Everyone was asking, what is your major? What do you want to do when you graduate? I had no idea. I had spent a night shadowing one of my best friends' moms who was a labor and delivery nurse early that summer. I saw many births and thought that was quite amazing. I remember standing at the end of one woman's hospital bed as I saw my first birth. I literally could not stop crying at the beauty and miracle of someone giving birth. But after having grown up spending way too much time in hospitals, I had not considered nursing. I will never forget a question that my resident assistant, April, had asked me around this time: "Heather, where does your greatest desire and talent meet the world's greatest need?" This really brought me back to listen to my deepest desires and to God. I will never forget this question. It's so profound to me that a simple question can help us access things so deeply. I find myself asking this question to myself and others often.

My Grandma Esther was a nurse and mom was a nurse, but I really had not considered it before that point. In fact, I remember saying as I began college, "I don't know what I am going to do, but I will not be a nurse." I saw the toll it took on the RN's that I knew. But it did seem that nursing fit the question that April had asked me. I took classes in just about every major in my freshman and sophomore years. When I arrived in Panama City beach for this 10-week discipleship training where I was learning about studying the Bible, sharing my faith, and prayer, I prayed quite a crazy prayer as a new person of faith. I prayed, "God, if you want me to be a nurse, will you send nurses into my life?" Well, in the following two weeks, I "randomly" met 18 nurses! Of course, it was not random! I knew it was God bringing those nurses across my path. They were on the beach, in restaurants, and they came into my check out line where I worked as a cashier at Publix. Not only was I meeting nurses, but I was meeting nurses who *loved* nursing and were ecstatic to encourage me to pursue it!

I was floored, and I journaled about every encounter, mainly thinking people would not believe me that I was meeting all of these nurses. Even once the beach project was over and I was back at Berry College and found out there was no nursing major offered at my college, I almost decided to pursue another major just to stay at Berry. All my friends and mentors were there, and I didn't want to leave. On the last day to change my classes, I went to Wendy's Restaurant, and of course, there were two more nurses there, and then I went to a bookstore off campus, and met yet *another* nurse. It was one of those times where God made the direction I was to take *super clear*!

I knew I could not get into any high-ranking nursing school with the grades I had made my freshman year after my head injury. I decided to shadow a nurse at a local neonatal ICU and she told me about Georgia Baptist College of Nursing (GBCN) in downtown Atlanta. This is where one of my best friend's mom had gone to nursing school when we were growing up. She said it was the best nursing school in the Southeast, super hard to get into, and the only school that had a full 3 years of clinical (hands-on training). She gave me the number of her "friend" at the school, and I called.

This friend of hers that I called happened to be an *admissions recruiter* and she said she was coming to Berry the following week and we could meet! What? She told me on the phone that there was a long waiting list and it was extremely competitive. Sure enough, when Lynn came to campus, she saw my grades and told me there was no way I could come there.

I told her my story of how God had shown me that I was to be a nurse, and I told her I understood she could not accept me, but I would be in nursing school somewhere. She once again apologized and said with my 1.7 GPA my freshman year and not having taken the right classes anyways, that it was impossible. I understood.

During that meeting, she said she had to make a phone call. She came back to the room in the student center literally minutes later, this being in October of my Junior year, and she said, "Heather, you are accepted into our school. You need to decide if you want to come in January or next fall!" I was floored and in tears. I said to her that I didn't understand because I had not even applied yet, and what about my grades? She just said, "We are inviting you to come." I knew the only explanation for this was that God had opened this door wide open *again*!

So after talking to my resident director and my bosses for my other on campus jobs, I was told to "go for it!" I was an RA at that point on a freshman hall, and it was so awesome to be able to drop some classes and finish out that time at Berry College in the middle of my junior year, really investing in friendships and in the freshmen on my hall. I was already petrified to leave this bubble of Berry College in rural Georgia and head to downtown Atlanta! But I knew it was meant to be.

Following God to Nursing School

It was always so tender of God to lead me as a new Christian in such a clear way. GBCN (it wasn't really a Baptist school at the time I went but it was founded on Biblical principles) was an all female school at that point, and I lived in the dorm in downtown Atlanta with some amazing women, some of whom are my closest friends today!

Classes were right downstairs in the same building. Sometimes we would go to class in our pj's, slippers and with blankets.

My new friend Joanna and I started a Bible study early on after transferring there in my dorm room about learning the names of God. It was such a gift to live in a dorm with all women studying nursing. I had to work *extra* hard in all of my classes. Having no memory and not being able to sleep, it made all things in life hard, but nursing school was so challenging to all of us and I often wondered if I would make it through. Staying up all night preparing for classes or clinicals was the norm for me.

The whole first year I was dreading going into care for

39

patients. As I learned nursing skills on mannequins, I shook like crazy and would go blank all of the time. I thought to myself, *how am I going to care for real people? Why did I do this? I am scared to death.*

I will never forget standing outside of my first real patient's door in the hospital for a very long time, with my instructor urging me each time she went down the hall and passed me. She finally pushed me through the patient's doorway and held it shut from the outside! Yes, I was pushing on the door handle trying to get out!

This precious patient called out "Hello, is someone there?" In a shaking voice I said, "Yes, this is Heather, your nursing student. I am here to help you in any ways that I can." She was a blind woman with a smile and with such kindness that I will never forget her. Surprisingly, her main request during that morning was that we sing "Amazing Grace" together. We sang with all of our hearts, I was in tears and she was grasping my hand. That moment seemed so much more significant than changing her bed, taking her vitals, or helping with her bath.

My very tall, seemingly intimidating nursing instructor who graduated from Harvard, poked her head in and just gave me a smile. This whole experience was such a gift. This sweet patient, whose room I was petrified to walk into, had been the *one* to really draw out my heart and voice!

I was so thankful for my mentor named Skip, who I met in my senior year of nursing school. She really encouraged me that true learning comes after you graduate. When I heard this, I felt like a pressure valve was released in me. I didn't have to remember everything I was learning! Hearing this really gave me a different perspective and she also helped my faith grow a ton. We always talked about how she had "free meddling rights" in my life which meant that she could ask me anything at any point. For example, if she tried to contact me late at night and could not reach me, she was quick to ask what was going on. She never held back. She always wanted to hear my true and authentic voice about everything I was going through. This accountability from another nurse and someone who had such wisdom and integrity (and, side note, is absolutely hilarious) was such a gift to me.

I graduated with honors from nursing school, which felt miraculous! I went from being a junior at Berry College, back to being a freshman at my nursing school. I dealt with intense anxiety with clinicals and also with performing my nursing skills in the lab. I had a huge fear of failure and had to work three times as hard as every other student because of my head injury. I felt like an imposter, like I couldn't do it. But God gave grace for each trial and each day.

A unique experience during nursing school and after was having the honor of being a doula (birthing companion) for some of my close friends. Later, I was trained as an official doula, and I can honestly say that being alongside women while they are giving birth has been such a heart and life transforming experience. Whether it's been a literal birth, or a doula of sorts to what God wants to birth through my friends in a spiritual sense, it is an honor to be a helper in this way.

Moving from rural Rome, GA, where Berry College was located, to downtown Atlanta for my nursing school, is when I fell in love with being in the city and really investing deeply in where I was planted. I also grew to have a love and concern for those from low-income communities and the unhoused. One day, when leaving my dorm, I saw a woman at the bus stop who was left there after being released from the ER in a wheelchair and was still in her hospital gown (our dorm was attached to the hospital). I knew I could not just pass her. She needed help. I could clearly see she was suffering from so much pain, mentally and physically, and I wanted to help in any way I could. I was thankfully able to get her into a shelter. I will never walk past a person, no matter if they are without a home or if they are millionaires, without really seeking to *see* the person and the heart that is in front of me.

When I started nursing school, someone challenged me to care for each person and each patient, as if it was Jesus himself laying in that hospital bed. The same went for any person that was in my presence, and that challenge is still in my mind every day: being fully present to whomever is in my path and loving with all that I am.

Learning from Missions

I also had a huge heart and desire to live overseas as a missionary for so much of my adult life. I almost moved into a refugee community in an apartment complex in Atlanta. But a relationship with a guy changed that plan. This was a season that happened post nursing school, where I first thought I might be heading towards marriage in a relationship. At least this is what was brought up often by the guy. I was preparing to move into a refugee apartment complex with two other women, and at the same time, this guy expressed his feelings for me. He was a guy my future roommate was interested in, and I had no idea. Beginning to date this guy caused a huge rift in that friendship, and we did not move into the apartment complex. It was one of the first times in my life when a big group of people were very unhappy with me.

The one gal shared with many others about her hurt and disapproval of my decisions and it caused a ton of pain to me. I had very few people to talk to about this and ended up confiding in and listening more to the voice of the guy I was dating than I did to my own voice and heart. Being so misunderstood during this situation was so hard, and there were many nights when I cried myself to sleep. I believe I found a security and a lifeline in being liked and pursued by this guy and it was quite confusing for him when I began pulling away from this relationship as an emotional intimacy had been built quickly and deeply because we were facing this conflict together. Breaking up with this guy, because I was unsure if I was ever supposed to get married, was confusing for both of us. It was also a lonely time, as I had lost a good number of friendships at the church we were both at from the break up and from the conflict that came from not moving into the refugee apartment. I was quite lonely. Thankfully, I did eventually reconcile with the gal that I ended up not moving in with.

My voice was really shaped and drawn out through being discipled as a new Christian and discipling others and even going with Campus Outreach to Japan, and after nursing school having life-changing times going to Brazil, Honduras, Guatemala, Mexico, Colombia, and North Africa. I was seen as a leader on these trips and was entrusted to invest in others on the trips. Even in doing short-term mission trips, my voice was shaped so much in these trips because all of the comforts of home and the security of the familiar was not there. I expressed to my teammates all the fears and feelings that were coming up inside of me, and through that vulnerability, they also expressed what they were feeling. It was life giving!

In a completely different experience, one group that I went on a vision trip with was made up of a team that functioned with no grace towards one another. The team was at each other's throats for every little thing. There were fights often and people felt judged and scared to speak up. It was like military training. I was supposed to be on staff with this group training college students for 18 months, but I am so glad I went on a 10-day vision trip first, because seeing how a team functioned without grace towards one another made it very clear that this was not for me. A vision trip was something I chose to do to check things out with this organization before making a long-term commitment. I felt comfortable using my voice with the students on that trip, but with staff there was no room for my voice. It was a challenging 10 days to say the least. I got to use my fear, insecurity, and love to pour into the students that were there.

43

My whole heart felt shut down when engaging with the staff, but I sure did journal a ton! This group has done much good in so many people's lives, and I am glad it exists, but it was not a good fit for me. It was also not the first, nor the last time, that I thought I was going to go overseas for a longer period and didn't.

I didn't return with this specific group to this hard region of the world, but I got to go join another family after my time studying counseling, and I *loved* it! They were a family so focused on grace and truly living out the gospel. They assumed the best of each other and knew that they were truly in this to reflect God's love to anyone who crossed their paths. Each of these short trips taught me so much about myself and about the utter importance of the physical, emotional, relational,and spiritual health both of those I was going to serve with and of myself! I saw and visited so many missionary teams that were so deeply struggling within themselves and with each other. I do know that had I gone to any of these places long term, I would have added to that unhealthiness.

The gift in these short trips was that I had more space to journal my raw thoughts and feelings, more time to share with my fellow teammates, and more time to tap into this deeper desire to use the talents and gifts I had to share with people that were different from me. My whole world view was expanding as I saw God's work in different people groups, and I realized how *big* the world is and how *small* my understanding of God is as well. I saw a deep, heart-level thankfulness among people that were living in the poorest of situations, and it was humbling.

I began to see during these trips the incredible privilege I had and also the deep biases and pride in my own heart. I really thought that I could "help" other people and that I was some sort of expert or had answers to things. I quickly began to feel that those I was meeting were the experts and I was there to learn and be humbled. My worldview was so small, and these trips blew my heart wide open to learn from others! I also came face to face again with my fear and insecurities, and thankfully, among my teammates, I was not the only one experiencing this. We had times where we could share vulnerably with each other.

I see now that these trips were so much more about shaping my heart and humbling me than they were about what I could offer as a counselor or nurse. Singing with the kids with my broken Spanish in Guatemala or Honduras, climbing Mt. Fuji in Japan while taking one breath at a time and thinking I wasn't going to make it, struggling so hard in North Africa trying to even get a basic grasp of Arabic was all so humbling. I remember feeling so insecure every day, but barely ever speaking about it to others.

I have seen through all of these experiences and trips that my main role is to listen to the voices of others and to learn, not to speak much. Whether it be the long-term missionaries that I was joining and serving or the people that were local to that area. I always thought I was called to be a long-term missionary overseas, but each time I have sought to head overseas, that door has shut, and an opportunity in the states opened.

Deciphering Life After College

As I was finishing nursing school, I was faced with yet more big decisions: going on staff with campus outreach, working at a hospital, working in a clinic, or going overseas. I journaled myself in circles. I felt so strongly that there was a right and wrong way to go. I did not understand that I could trust my heart and the desires that God had placed in my heart and take a step. I was often paralyzed by the fear of making the "wrong" decision.

As I re-read my journal, I could see the anguish over big decisions. My journals were full of page after page of agonizing over what God's will was, especially in regard to relationships and life decisions. Oh, how I wish I did not take myself or these decisions so seriously. I would "over-spiritualize" every decision in the moment. When I look back now, I see they were not a big deal at all. I could have walked forward in many different paths, and enjoyed and honored God, no matter the decision! Finally, I took some steps forward.

After graduating nursing school, I had the dream job of continuing to live in the dorm while working for the admissions office to help bring in the new class of freshmen. I also worked at a clinic in Atlanta. I will share more about that later. This was a special year of getting to live in the dorm in the city for almost no money *and* working as a nurse.

I was *petrified* and so insecure being a new nurse. With my lack of sleep, poor memory, self doubt and fear of failure, I wrote myself "truth reminders" that I could hang in my shower and read every morning. I found these in my journals. How quickly I have always forgotten the unwavering love of God for me, no matter what I am doing or what others think of me. I did this because I got so distracted by the opinions of others or even my own fears! These truth letters kept me grounded as I read them every day when I showered. I had put them in a plastic covering so that I could literally read them every day. They were used to draw me back to God and to a more grounded place throughout the days that were quite hard. Especially being a new nurse, and scared to death, so unsure of myself and my skills as a nurse, I needed some reminders of the bigger picture—of God's heart for me and what my life was truly about.

One letter I wrote to myself in the fall of 2000 was exactly this. I wrote this just as I was graduating from nursing school.

"Heather, remember today that God has a plan for you. He wants you to let go of control and completely trust Him with every aspect of your day! Remember today that Jesus died for you Heather and rose again to pay for all of your sin so that you can have a relationship with God that is free, abundant and intimate. Look around today and watch as God is pursuing your heart! Look at His creation, His provision. Look at who He is and the people He has placed in your life. Remember today that there is nothing that comes into your life that God doesn't know all about and allow. He is sovereign and He uses all things together for your good. He desires for you to have intimacy with Him today in every way. Live today to the fullest because it could be your last. Make the most of every opportunity and seek to share Christ and His amazing love with everyone who crosses your path. Seek to really know who God is and love Him with your whole heart. Seek to really know the hearts of people around you and really love them with the love of Christ. God I am here not to be known, honored or glorified- I am here to be Your vessel, to be used by You so that You may receive Glory through me. Oh God, I pray that I would walk today taking each step very aware of my need for You, very aware of who I am as Your loved child, very aware of how You want to use me in others' lives. Whether they be family, friend, foe or stranger. God show me where You want me to go and how I should spend each minute of this day as I walk in love with You. Help me to remember today that this life is like a drop in the ocean compared to eternity. Please Father fix my eyes and heart not on earthly pleasures but on my rewards in heaven. Fix my heart on what is on Your heart- You, Your Word and the souls of women and men. Teach me how to be faithful in the small things of today, to be a wise steward of all that is entrusted to me and to have a simplified life. Help me to be like Mary today, resting at the feet of Jesus, worshiping Him and entrusting all desires, dreams, worries and cares to Him. Please help me to not do anything today out of duty but to do only the things You lay on my heart to do with the motive of love and serving You. I pray today Father that You would make me more like

Christ. Please reveal any sin in my life and quickly break my heart and bring me to repentance. Thank you Father, for a relationship with You that is joyful, abundant, exciting and awesome. I love You. Help me to leave the past behind me, be fully in the moment with You now and trust the future completely to You!"

Learning to listen deeply to God, my own soul cries, and to my close community prepared me to take some big steps in the seasons that followed. I saw that my worth could not come from pleasing others or from being liked. So many of my decisions, even this early on in life, were not approved of or understood by the people in my life. Even so, I can also see now that throughout these experiences, my voice was slowly growing and starting to come out more authentically, albeit very slowly and with much hesitancy, at this point in my life.

CHAPTER 4

VOICING BOUNDARIES

I NEVER REALLY LEARNED AS A YOUNG GAL or even through my college years how to say "no" to the needs/wants of others, whether with family, friends, boyfriends (more on this later), or even strangers. I even remember just standing and listening as a male extended family member visited us in Georgia during middle school while he told me I was fat and ugly and that my braces really made my cheeks fat. No one else was around. I carried that so long, and in some ways, it still impacts me to this day. I felt that I just needed to agree with people and say "yes," and that likely I was wrong if I thought about saying "no." I thought that my gut was not to be trusted, even if on the inside it seemed to be yelling, "NO!"

Throughout my life, with the training I have had in being a counselor, spiritual director, nurse, and life coach along with being a people pleaser, it has been extra hard to learn how to say "no." It seems when I finally found the courage to say "no," I was often met with resistance or even rejection. I remember even in high school trying to find my "no" in a dating relationship and it was constantly questioned. This made me question it myself. It has also been hard to ask for and accept the help I need for myself whether it be emotionally, mentally, physically, financially, or relationally.

In 2005, while working in a clinic for the underserved in Atlanta, I realized that my bigger passion than nursing was to connect with the heart of my patients. Don't get me wrong, I always loved being able to help relieve a physical ailment, but I enjoyed listening and hearing my patients' stories and life experiences even more. Sometimes I would even get in trouble with the management at that clinic about taking too much time in people's clinic rooms and slowing the patient flow.

I wanted to study counseling to not only understand the working of other people's hearts, but my own heart as well. So this is why I decided to move to Philly to go to Seminary to study counseling. I had read the book, *Instruments in the Redeemer's Hands*, by Paul Tripp, and I wanted to study at the school where he taught. Finding my "no" at the clinic where I was currently working in Atlanta while knowing it was time to move on was so hard. I knew deep in my soul though that it was time. I agonized over making decisions, especially big ones like this one. I visited a couple of schools and I was drawn to Christian Counseling Education Foundation (CCEF) in Philadelphia for many reasons, but the main one was the book I mentioned above. Thankfully when I visited, I got to meet with a few professors, sit in on a class, and ask the questions that were helping me to discern where I was being called. I wanted to know my own heart better through studying counseling while also learning how to really draw out the hearts of others.

I had also made an amazing connection with Nina when I visited. She was a student at Westminster who was preparing to go to North Africa with her family. I had been on a short trip to North Africa before that and wanted to go back.

While visiting the counseling training in Philly, I got to stay with Nina and her family and really connected with them. My hope in going to seminary was to prepare me for the mission field overseas. And the more specific reason I wanted to study counseling was that I had heard that more missionaries were leaving the mission field because of interpersonal conflict with other missionaries than for any other reason. I thought maybe I could be trained to meet with teams to help them resolve conflict overseas and be of assistance in helping them stay.

Holy No's

During seminary, I mostly lived in community with a 3-generation family and one other single gal. It was so life-giving to live with this family and be a part of having shared dinners and the sharing of our lives in the day-to-day. I worked at Esperanza Health Center with two of my roommates and we often could share our burdens with one another as we drove to and from work. I was thankful as well to have Lucy and Angel (I called them my Philly mama and daddy) and they sure took care of me and the other single gal who lived there. Living with two children also taught me so much about family and the importance of having a "village" to raise kiddos. They are dear to me and the love they poured out on both Ana and I was healing as well as fun! Taking turns cooking for one another and sharing about our days became the norm of each day. It was in the backyard of this big, shared house where I got married in 2012!

During seminary, I quickly discovered while writing self-reflection papers for my counseling classes that I needed just as much help as others do and that accepting that help, in my own life, is way harder than giving help. I still have so far to go in using my voice to ask for help and using my voice to say "no," when so often I say "yes" because it is so deeply ingrained in me as the "loving" thing I can do. Sometimes "yes's" can be super unloving and selfish.

While writing this book, I was reading some books and listening to YouTube videos by a well known doctor whose name is Dr. Mate. Dr. Mate talks about the actual power of saying, "no." Beginning to learn late in life how to say "no" has helped me find more health. I am more authentic and intentional in finding my voice and speaking it. Dr. Mate shares in his book called, *The Myth of Normal*, to ask ourselves, "Where this week did I have a hard time saying 'no'?" and "When did I want to say 'no,' but I didn't say it?" There is such tension in disappointing others, but it's really my own fear in disappointing someone or being rejected. This has been a trajectory of my life in jobs, relationships, and commitments. In not saying "no," it has led to exhaustion, confusion in relationships, and maybe even worse, illness. The word "no" still does not show up often in my life.

My mentor Ellen has always said, "we have got to say Holy 'no's,' so that we can say 'yes' to the very few things we are called to." I think I will go to my grave seeking to learn this and to let go of seeking to please others.

Speaking to Please

For me, my words are often influenced by what I think people think of me. I remember it hitting home when someone told me at one point, "What others think of me is none of my business." Wow!

I hesitate sometimes in speaking my true heart or need out of fear of rejection or disapproval. This causes me at times to edit my voice, even if just a little, or sometimes completely! This even means at times that I do not listen to what I truly need or what my body (especially with the illnesses that I deal with) needs at any given time. It can be dangerous. My FOMO (fear of missing out) or my people-pleasing tendency can really hinder me from being radically honest with others and even with myself. This has been something I have wrestled with my whole life, and no doubt will continue to work through and need help with.

I stand in awe of people in my life, or those that I read or watch, that can speak their truth no matter what people around them think or say. They seem so free! (At this moment I am thinking about the author and speaker, Kate Bowler). I remember reading the book by Ed Welch, who was one of my teachers when I studied counseling, called: *When People are Big, and God is Small*. That title! So much of this book resonated deep within my soul. I remember a key takeaway for my heart was that it seems the voice/opinion of others has more weight or influence than the voice of God at times. That the reality of what others think seems so much stronger or *bigger* than the opinion of God about what I am doing, thinking or saying.

A quote that hit me by Welch was about "regarding other people, our problem is that we need them (for ourselves) more than we love them (for the glory of God)." But as I learn more and more who I am, my voice becomes more authentically my own and is not morphed or edited by what people think.

When I arrived in Philadelphia for seminary, I was so exhausted from pleasing people and not having healthy boundaries. I had worked so hard in Atlanta and then made this huge move. Leaving everything that was familiar and everyone I knew. In a very short period of time, I had also been to North Africa twice, Honduras, Guatemala, Japan, Mexico and later Colombia for short trips. All of this while dealing with some chronic illnesses that had become a big part of my story. Beginning with my head injury, I stopped sleeping and after that many other illnesses came. All of these illnesses have helped me to slow down in different seasons of my life which all have been very much needed, though I did not feel that way in the moment. They have also helped me to listen more deeply to my body and to the voice that God has given me. Voicing boundaries and learning to trust our own inner voice is for our own good and the good of the world!

CHAPTER 5

USING MY VOICE FOR GOOD

IN SO MANY OF THE EXPERIENCES that I share about in this book, I realized that my voice could be used for good, for change in the world and for the voiceless. I realized that most people don't want unsolicited advice, or to be told what to do; they know what they need to do and what is best for them. I'm finding that most people just want to be listened to, really deeply heard and loved right where they are. I desire this so deeply in my own life. I realized the quote "people don't care what you know, they just want to know that you care," is *oh-so* true!

This was also shaped in me most by being trained as a spiritual director. I pursued this training after I attended seminary. Being a spiritual director means meeting with people and seeking to listen deeply to what God is doing in their souls, and to provide a safe place to encounter God in unique ways. I had already finished my counseling training when I pursued becoming a spiritual director, but in being a spiritual director, or "soul companioning" as I like to call it, I have really changed. While doing this, I am not in advice or "fix it" mode. I am a witness to and holding space for what is being birthed in others, being there to draw out the deep work that is happening inside someone's soul and to celebrate with them. Other times it means being with someone who is deeply grieving or may feel very far from God and allowing that to be without seeking to change anything or anyone. Also, seeking out soul companioning for myself has been transformative for allowing my raw and unfiltered voice to really be heard and honored.

In providing spiritual direction, people have asked over and over for a non-judgemental space where they can say anything and know that I will *not* try to fix them. Me saying things like "That sounds like it is a tough situation. How can I support you? I am here to listen. That sounds hurtful. I know you know what is best for you in this situation," and just being a witness to what someone is walking through without trying to help or change it, can be the *most* helpful thing. My main role was helping people listen to their *own* hearts and to the heart of God. I felt a bit like a matchmaker, connecting people to the love that God has for them.

I am thinking about one person who said she wanted to come to meet with me. She said on the phone before we even began to meet, "I do not want to be told what to do, judged, or fixed, but just want to be heard. *Truly* heard" (This is challenging as a helper and a counselor but being a spiritual companion is so different from counseling). For another gal, she communicated best through her art. So I would have a pad of paper and some colored pencils. During the beginning of our time spent in silence, she would often create some thing in the form of an elaborate drawing, and then at times share its significance with me. These were all holy ground moments. I saw that people felt loved and accepted right where they were and I prayed that they would truly feel the love of God as we met together. What an honor. My true desire in all things is to be used by God to be His gentle hands, heart, and voice of love to all who cross my path.

Everyday Interactions

I have learned throughout this journey that I can use my voice to seek to turn someone's day around (hopefully for the better) in *every* interaction I have. Whether it be people I know like family, neighbors, friends, or patients or even strangers in the store, health care providers, people at a drive-thru, customer service on the phone, pharmacy workers, or whoever I encounter (including people who are the grumpiest), my goal has always been to help make their days better and to love well. We literally have no idea what the person in front of us is facing or walking through.

One odd thing about my life experience since becoming a nurse has been that I often am faced with other people's medical crises or incidents outside of the clinic or hospital. It is uncanny the number of flights I have been on when a medical professional is needed, or the sheer number of times that I have come upon a car accident or someone in the grocery store passing out. Usually, I find my voice is needed to bring comfort to a person, or to direct people around me to know what to do.

It even happened in a grocery store this week as I am writing this chapter. A woman collapsed and it turned out she was diabetic, and her blood sugar was low. I find it ironic that I am not an ER nurse, nor do I like emergency situations at all, but somehow (by the grace of God and a rush of adrenaline) I always know what to do. This time it was getting someone else to go get a glucometer (blood sugar meter) from the pharmacy, getting her some milk, getting her information in case she lost consciousness and providing comfort to her while her blood sugar came back up. We were able to get a family member there to help her as well. I always saw my mom responding to medical situations growing up, but never thought I would one day walk in her footsteps.

Close Friends Speaking Into My Life

I have also experienced the power of when someone else feels comfortable to speak their truth and use their voice no matter how it is perceived or received. I remember sitting in a small group in Philly at my new church shortly after I had moved there for seminary and our leaders were so real, vulnerable, and authentic with their voice. I will never forget one of the first gatherings I was at. I will call them Samatha and Darren. They shared very openly about the ways they were struggling in their marriage. Samantha shared so openly with the whole group in front of Darren. I was floored! Darren was totally fine with it. I kept watching his face to see if he would be upset. You mean, it was OK and even welcome to share our vulnerable struggles with a trusted group? I had *no* idea! I never saw that nor was I taught that this was OK while growing up. I felt so free, and it gave me the permission to be more real, open and vulnerable too. What a slow, long and sometimes painful journey that has been, but what a gift!

Another friend (I call her my "heart friend") and I would spend up to five hours a week with one another on Monday afternoons for a season of my life. I am so grateful for this friendship, and she always speaks her truth. We are both Enneagram 2's (referred to as "the helper") and she has a heart of gold! She is one of those friends that always comes bearing a meal, or some homemade chocolate and peanut butter dessert (my favorite). We have shared deep matters of the heart for over 25 years now. One recent afternoon, I saw that she had a tattoo. I was surprised. It was so powerful hearing that this tattoo symbolized finding her voice and truly speaking it, even though what she had to speak was hard. What a story. Her tattoo symbols mean "God is greater than any mountain top experience and any valley experience." She found her voice by getting a tattoo and saw it as an expression of her overcoming the opinions of others, knowing that above and beyond any circumstance, any harsh word, any mistakes or failings, God will always love her for who she is.

I did the same in getting my own tattoo with a different friend, my "Budsie." It was *her* idea, and it was a quick decision for me (side note, I *shocked* my little brother when I called him from the tattoo parlor because he had always wanted one and I had talked him out of it). The reason I got it was that I have always been so worried that due to my head injury I would not remember my life or that I would lose the details of how things have played out. I was always told that I could not do this or that, and getting a tattoo was one of them. My dear Budsie and I went together to get tattoos that really have deep significance for us. Mine is the Greek symbol for "manna" which means God will provide what we need for each day. Although the tattoo was not celebrated by all of my people, it was a way that I could use my voice and also be reminded for the rest of my life that God would provide what I needed at the exact moment I needed it. That I would always have enough.

I also think about my best friend Amanda using her voice when she could barely speak because of her cancer. She literally brought comfort to all who came into her presence. She would often say, I see Jesus and He is near. Fast forward to 2015 and the same was true of Rebecca. She also had cancer, and this is one of those ladies that just radiated joy no matter what. Her voice was always one that made you feel safe, heard, loved, and celebrated. I saw the same persevering perspective in one of my close friends Jessica who had had cancer 5 times and she was my age—in her 40's as well. She had the hardest life circumstances I had ever seen, especially while sick, but I was blown away the last time I visited with her before she passed, and she had the most radiant peace and joy amid excruciating pain. The same was true of Jane (known as

59

Nightbirde when she sang). Her words cut to the core. She was on the television show, America's Got Talent (AGT), and I was in awe from the first minute a friend sent me her performance of "It's OK." I started to listen deeply to her voice each time she would show up on Instagram or put out a new song. It was always profound and brought me to tears.

Each of these ladies battled cancer well and are with Jesus now, but I can tell you they still almost daily have some sort of impact on my life and undoubtedly so many others. I miss all of them and they are missed by many. There is something that comes with suffering that brings a rawness, a vulnerability, and a refreshing sense of truth that penetrates my own soul and I think had an impact on everyone else who knew them, too. One of our neighbors that we are super close to was recently diagnosed with uterine cancer and she has lost five family members to cancer. We are seeking to walk with her and her family during this time and my heart is so tender at what the outcome could be, but hoping and praying that the chemotherapy works for her!

In being mentored through campus outreach, in nursing school, in seminary and even now, each of these women's voices, among many others, have been used to transform me and help me learn to grow in confidence in using my own voice. I will never forget when one mentor, Ellen, gathered two other women when I was in a destructive dating relationship, and they called me on Skype and really spoke boldly, without fear of how I would respond or what I would say. Ellen's voice has been used over and over throughout the years, to not only help me see more clearly, but to find and celebrate the voice God has given me. The amazing mentors and close chicas (a group of ten ladies that have shared life for over fifteen years) in my life have been some of the most powerful tools to help me know God's voice and my own, and I am forever grateful. They don't use pat answers, they show up when I am at my worst and so incredibly sick or downright cranky and have spoken truth and loved me through it. I don't feel like I must "get it together" or answer "fine" when they ask how I am. These ladies keep their word, are faithful friends, and consistently show up! I am so grateful.

Keeping Our Word

I sure learned in the beginning of my faith journey through campus outreach, and continuing since then, the power of using our voice to speak our word and commitment to others. I have seen that this is, in a sense, integrity. I really have sought, as much as possible, to use my voice to speak my honest intentions and desires. To speak my commitment to others whether it be a small thing or a big thing. A small example of when I use my voice is that I will meet a person at a certain time, and I plan to keep that commitment and feel it's unloving of me to not keep that commitment of time (unless of course I am living in a country that does not see time in that way or if an unpreventable occurrence happens). A bigger example is using my voice and my words to speak my vows to my husband before God and our loved ones. With all of my heart, I desire to keep these words/vows of my heart to my husband.

We all fail at the reality of keeping our word and using our voice for good every day in some way. When I become aware of it, I seek to go to the person, apologize and ask for forgiveness. I also have had a super hard time when commitments are made to me, or things are promised, and then it can seem like it's no big deal for that promise to not be kept.

In my adult life, I have been super hurt by being told how valuable I am and how I am wanted and desired for who I am, but at times when I show up with needs and with who I truly am, there have been times when I have been completely rejected or ghosted. This has reinforced this sense that my needs are too much, that I am too much. The lesson being that I should not share or speak vulnerably who I am or what I need. *Ugh.*

For example, there was a time when Jer and I lived with some people and one person was not appropriate with me. It took a while to build up courage to say something, but when I finally spoke up, I was immediately not believed and was evicted from this place of living. This had been a place where I had been showered with so much love, words, hugs, flowers, gifts, and time. Sometimes I was teased and sometimes even harassed when I did not do exactly as this person commanded. It took so much bravery to speak up about the hard things, and then to be shut down, not believed, and immediately kicked out of the home and their lives. It really had an impact on me, and still does.

After it all happened, I went into a bout of depression. I even doubted for a while if I should have spoken up, but I am so glad I did. Even though I have forgiven this person, it still impacts me to this day. How does one go from saying, "I love you so much" one day, to the next day saying, "get out of my house in two hours and I do not care where you go"? We had no sustainable employment at that time, as I was too sick to work. Jer was working some temp jobs while looking for an engineering job day and night.

Those types of words, reneging of love and commitment, or even dismissing a desire to work things out, is a wound, and in my experience it was traumatic. I wonder how many women out there have never been able to speak about what has happened to them out of sheer fear, to anyone, much less the one who has betrayed them. I sadly get it.

Growing up in the South, there have been many times when people have committed and said one thing to me out loud, and then I found out what they really wanted or desired from me or even thought of me was completely different than what was communicated. There was an example even the week I was writing this. I was staying with some people with whom I was invited and welcomed like family. I had been told that I was welcome to stay until a certain date. It took a lot of planning to work out where to go and how to get around after the time that I was going to leave there. Well, the hostess messaged and basically said, I need you to get out of living here and leave the car you are borrowing within two days. I was so disoriented and confused not only by the reneging on the word and the promise, but the way in which I was told. It's a feeling of being so easily disposed of, or that my needs, feelings or emotions do not matter or are too much, and that is a lie. Having needs is being whole and human.

There is always a need for me to forgive those who have hurt me in these ways, and to ask for forgiveness for not keeping my word or speaking what I really mean or need as well. There is also a place to stand up and share with others what is hurtful, and that is where I deeply struggle. I guess if I am being ruthlessly honest, I wonder if I am worth it.

Esperanza Health Clinic

When I moved to Philly in 2005 to go to seminary to study counseling, I also worked at a clinic called Esperanza Health Center and did home visits with people living with HIV. I got to be an advocate in very practical ways for others that were sick. This was deeply life changing. Not only was it quite a shift going from rural Georgia to Philadelphia, Pennsylvania, but to head into peoples' homes doing a type of nursing that was completely and totally new to me.

I remember a transformative moment after trying to do my job at Esperanza with my own strength, that I just gave up trying and fell on my face in tears. I wanted to quit. It felt impossible and caused so much anxiety and stress because I had no memory; I could not memorize the HIV meds like I needed to. I could not remember all that I needed to do for each patient. My level of exhaustion from not sleeping as well made it hard to function. This was also the time when my health really began to tank, but I was told over and over that I was fine. I was so exhausted in every way. I would lay my head on my desk in my office to just close my eyes. I would drink Coca-Cola every day just for energy to make it through. I felt almost lifeless—a shell of a human.

A turning point came one day as I drove around doing home visits. I often had music playing in my car to keep me awake or maybe distracted/numb from all that I was seeing around me in North Philly (I am an empath through and through). One day, in an almost audible sense in my heart, I felt as if God was calling me to turn the music off, to be alert, watching and prayerful as I drove around the city seeing my beloved patients in their homes. I was *floored* by how aware I became not only of all the brokenness around me in the streets (drugs, homelessness, prostitution, guns, violence, young kids walking alone and sometimes without shoes or proper clothing for the summer or winter), but I also felt my own brokenness and neediness in a whole new way. My car became a place where I began to pray daily for what I was seeing around me and in me, and I also began to listen more. Listening to God's voice and listening to the voice of my heart. My days as a nurse in North Philly and my heart for that city were forever changed from that day forward. Don't get me wrong, I still had days where I just wanted to numb, to not see or feel the brokenness in or around me, but God kept drawing me back for another day.

Even though I felt so clueless living in the Northeast, in a land so far from home and *oh-so* different. I was so glad to have the community of Esperanza Health Center where we began each day in worship and praying for each other. I also met some of my closest friends there and was so helped by being mentored by nurses that were already working there. But I was most impacted by my patients!

One patient, I will call Elsa, who was forced by her family to live in a shed behind her family's home. I was able to use my voice to educate her family. Her family was feeding her on paper plates and plastic utensils. She had to use the bathroom outside in a hole in the ground. This was 2006! They thought they could catch HIV just by sharing space with her or touching something that had touched her. I got to sit with her in her family's home and clarify the ways that HIV could be transmitted. Elsa was sitting next to me in tears.

I also had co-workers with HIV. One of them hugged someone in the kitchen at their church and the pastor said in front of the congregation, "You better get checked for HIV now that he hugged you!" The ignorance and the power of these hurtful words really tore these dear ones down.

I remember seeing my patient, "Adam," in the psych ward as he had not been doing well while not taking his medications and had been hearing voices due to his schizophrenia. I asked him when I visited, "What are the voices saying to you today?" He said, "They are telling me to kill you." I asked him what he was saying back to the voices, and he said, "I am thinking about it." I quickly told him that I had better go and exited. It was not his fault.

Home Visits

Doing home visits with HIV patients was so transformative for my heart, life and future. Realizing I was a guest that was being welcomed into peoples' homes for a vulnerable reason taught me so much about being a guest.

In doing home visits, sometimes there was so much stuff on the floor I could not see the actual floor but could only see mice moving the papers. Or I would see bugs crawling up the walls (or sometimes up my pants), and I really learned how not to react. This was a vulnerable situation for these patients, and I wanted them to feel honored by me and comfortable so that they could be honest with me and also feel the freedom to have me into their homes and lives as things really were, and not put on a show. They did not need to clean up for me. It reminded me of the love of God. We do not have to get cleaned up as we enter His presence. We are welcomed with loving open arms, as we are. The brokenness I saw around me was the same brokenness I faced in myself.

I was so humbled by my job at Esperanza. God definitely has a sense of humor and likes to surprise us, I think. One of my patient's sons was one of the biggest drug dealers in North Philly. He used his voice to share about me to the other drug dealers in the area and said if anything happened to me that they would have to deal with him. He *really* got upset at me when I changed my license plate from GA to PA without telling him ahead of time. He asked one day, "How am I supposed to protect you or have my people protect you if I don't know your license plate!??" Wow, I had no idea. Not once did anything happen to me in the nine years of doing home visits in North Philly.

There were several times when I would go out with the HIV outreach staff that did HIV testing around the city and sometimes we would go "under the bridge." This was a place where there were many people using heroin, prostitutes, and there were drug deals going on all around us. It had a potent smell of urine, and I wondered if some of the people whose legs were sticking out of the tents under the bridge were even alive. To say that my eyes were opened to whole new realities in this world was an understatement. But I met some of the most honest people who had faced some of the hardest life situations you could ever imagine. I can completely understand that people would want to use substances to numb the pain they had experienced. We all do the same with various things. I have no room to judge anyone *ever*. Knowing that my place in these situations was to listen, was paramount.

Advocating for Others

It sure took a *long* time for most of my patients to deeply trust me and for them to open up with their struggles. This trust was so precious to me and yet, I knew I would always be an outsider in a lot of ways. So helping to develop the Community Health Promoter program at the clinic was important to me. Each of us who helped to start this program realized that people from North Philly had a stronger voice in teaching about health issues to their neighbors. There was a *huge* impact by the voices of the hundreds of health promoters that are all throughout North Philly. They had a way bigger impact than I (especially as a white nurse from the south) could ever have.

One health promoter couple had a BBQ in their backyard and the husband spent time with the men in the backyard and talked about men's health and the wife was inside talking about other health issues with the women. It was a huge success! Another health promoter noticed the signs of a stroke that his neighbor was exhibiting. He took his neighbor's blood pressure and called 911. It was indeed a stroke. Things like this happened countless times. I realized that many people don't need to hear my voice, but to hear the voice of someone close to them who they trust. We can share our skills and training with others so that they can be equipped to use their voices in these types of situations.

During this season, I also worked for a while in home health and hospice and did that again in a season when I lived in the Raleigh/Durham area. Having seen the power of little ones coming into this world (as a prenatal nurse and doula before this time) and honoring the voices/desires of the women that were giving birth, was an amazing privilege. I can say it was just as much of a privilege to honor the voices/desires/wishes of those leaving this earth in their final days. I have been so moved to be alongside people in their journeys and really hearing and honoring their voices in the most vulnerable of times, in their giving birth, and also in their passing. Holding open, non-judgemental, loving space is what is desired and even required in these times. Oh, how my soul, and I think everyone's soul, desires this to be the case throughout their lives.

My job as an HIV nurse at Esperanza was in adherence, helping people to be consistent with their medications. I'd go to people's houses and set up pill boxes and other reminders to help them remember to take their meds. If their viral load of the HIV virus was down by taking their meds consistently, they could not spread HIV. Some would forget to take them, which was understandable, although I didn't really get that at the time and would sometimes feel frustrated with my patients. After I was sick for a while and had to take lots of meds for myself, I went back to some of my patients and apologized about how hard I was on them about them not taking their meds consistently. I had no idea how challenging it was.

When I had Lyme disease, I had to take up to 50 meds and supplements at a time, and I hated it. I cried at least twice a day when I sat down to look at my meds in the pill box. I never truly understood how hard taking all of those pills was until then. It even reminded me just how sick I was. The same was true for my patients. Some of them didn't want to acknowledge they had HIV, and taking those pills was a reminder. I tearfully apologized to these women that I had maintained contact with that I hadn't been more sensitive regarding taking medication. I am so thankful that we can use our voices to say, "I am sorry."

When I found my voice to apologize, it shifted my relationships with them. We are still friends on facebook. I got permission from the health center for this. It was really humbling to apologize, and I was in tears.

One patient I saw refused to take any of her meds. She said she would rather die. It reminded her every day that she had HIV. She didn't know her partner had it when he transmitted it to her, and it reminded her of how and when she found out. Of course, she didn't want to take them. I know I don't have HIV, but Lyme usually comes with needing to take a lot of meds and it's transmissible as well. It is *miserable* taking all those meds, and I had no idea. I jumped to so many conclusions before experiencing it myself. Even if I didn't voice my disapproval of people not taking their meds, I thought it and felt it in my heart, and you know they felt that from me! Sometimes, our actions speak so much louder than our words.

Sometimes it has been tricky to be both a patient and an RN. I learned that I had to use my voice both for myself and for other patients in one such situation. As a patient, I had been meeting with a doctor and I had to pay out of pocket for this treatment because of his specialty. A few weeks into meeting with this doctor I realized that the billing practices were not right. After being denied a conversation with this doctor about the funky billing practices, it took meeting with a different doctor in another state to finally get up the courage to report this previous doctor to the overseeing board of medicine. I could not imagine this happening to other people and the doctor in the other state convinced me it was my responsibility to report it to the board of medicine. I did this mere months before the pandemic began and so it took a long time for the report to get investigated, but there were disciplinary actions taken against this doctor. This was not something I wanted to do, having to speak up about someone who was doing something wrong, but it was something I felt needed to happen for the sake of all patients.

Drawing out the voice of others, speaking up for someone when their voice is not heard, and using my voice when it's *hard* to do so, are lessons that will leave me forever changed. Through learning this, I have also learned that even though there are many times when we can use our voice to love and serve others, sometimes there are times when it's just best not to speak at all. Our voice and our words can truly help and heal, or they can cause hurt.

CHAPTER 6

LISTENING SPEAKS
LOUDER THAN SPEAKING

I HAVE LEARNED SOMETIMES that it's best to *not* speak, but instead to just listen well to the voices of others. This was demonstrated and lived out through many people I know and has been shown in deeply practical ways through the Global Immersion Project (TGIP) when we moved to San Diego. We did immersion trips with TGIP to Israel and Palestine as well as down the road just 20 minutes from where we live to Tijuana, Mexico.

We were immersed in practicing this principle as well through living in an "intentional community" of faith in our neighborhood in San Diego. This was with a community of people in the Golden Hill neighborhood where we would live within walking distance of each other, meet multiple times a week for worship, do community dinners, have prayer walks, and invite neighbors and co-workers to join us in our everyday lives. I will never forget the first day we met Christiana (one of the leaders) to hear about this neighborhood church. We sat and talked for hours after walking with her about three blocks away to a quaint coffee shop. On the walk to the coffee shop, I think she spoke to more neighbors than most people talk to in a week! I am not kidding. A neighbor named Chris was delighted to see Christiana and stopped working in her garden to talk to her. People honked and waved at Christiana as we walked along. A houseless person who slept near Christiana's house had a question for her. Christiana knew several people even as we walked into the coffee shop. It went on and on. That's when I knew that what I'd read about this community before we visited, was really being lived out in practical ways. We had been yearning to learn from this community by becoming a part of it. We quickly noticed that one of the foundational ingredients to building meaningful relationships was by taking time to care and lovingly listen and learn. Being a part of this intentional community for a few years was the most powerful form of Church that I had ever experienced. We were so vulnerable with each other and really sought to build one another up. It was deeply transformative.

Everyday Peacemakers

This was a key time where both Jer and I learned to really listen to our own true voice, and the biggest gift to me in this season was that the community we were a part of really saw the value of each of our gifts. With sharing life so frequently and covenanting in community and relationship with these dear souls, there was a sense of truly drawing out our voices. It was safe with this group. I was most encouraged as the group really saw the value that Jer's heart, voice and leadership brings to all who know him. The leaders and our other community members sought to purposely encourage my dear introverted Jer to share his wisdom and use his voice. I was brought to tears so many times as they encouraged him to speak, and they were so impacted each time he did. This is what I *always* experience with Jer, but to see others really see the value in his voice and creatively draw it out meant *so* much to both of us, and especially to me.

He had heard me say countless times before this season how important his voice is, but to have the whole group affirm the same thing, it seems like he really began to believe it and to share more. All of us knew that we would be lacking if we did not hear his voice, and that is the same with each of our voices, gifts and perspectives. What a gift to experience such a *true* picture of the body of Christ!

A powerful comment from one of my community mates from 2015 that I am reminded of almost daily for myself or for others is when Emilie said to me, "Heather, go where you are celebrated, not where you are just tolerated." This statement has helped me see relationships that need to be let go of and ones that need to be pursued.

Sharing our life stories within this safe community, while walking in so much internal pain and toil, was so healing. We lived out together the pillars of the Global Immersion Project which so clearly reflect the heart of God. These pillars that I believe are so important that shaped our community and continue to be pillars that guide our life decisions are:

1) Everyday Peacemakers see the humanity, dignity, and image of God in everyone.
2) Everyday peacemakers move toward conflict with tools to heal rather than to win.
3) Everyday peacemakers contend, not by getting even, but by getting creative in love.
4) Everyday peacemakers share tables with former enemies and celebrate the big and small ways God is restoring our broken world.

Since 2014, I have believed these principles and strived to share life with people who walk out these principles in relationships with each other, neighbors, co-workers and in all situations of life—even very hard relationships. These principles have changed the way Jer and I live and interact with everyone. This complemented and enhanced what I had learned in my spiritual direction training. I have seen the deep value in listening very deeply and doing this way more often than I speak.

Listening Takes Time

This practice of deep listening was also formed in me while studying counseling in seminary. I will never forget shadowing Dr. Tripp and at about six weeks into him counseling a young boy, I and other students asked in the debriefing time after one session, "Why are you going so slowly with this kid in counseling? It seems like you aren't getting anywhere!" I will never forget Dr. Tripp's response. He said that we had to keep in mind that he "did not even know this kid for a total of an average workday yet." This lesson from Dr. Tripp and the kid he counseled really hit me. Even though they had been meeting for 6 weeks, Dr. Tripp reminded us that he had only known this kid for 6 hours. It was so impactful to me to take the time needed to really hear a person, get to know who they truly are and wait to gain the trust to be able to speak.

This was lived out on a day-to-day basis and also tested when we moved into new neighborhoods like Germantown in Philly and in San Diego. We needed to not speak for a while; we needed to listen. For example, getting to know Mily and sitting at her feet and learning about her Latine culture, being invited into her home on Christmas Eve and sharing life in the day to day, has shown me so much about my own privilege and lack of deep understanding of the suffering of others. Or in South Atlanta when I worked at the clinic after nursing school. There I had the privilege of sitting at the feet of our African American neighbor, Ms. P and learning about the neighborhood by sitting at her feet on the ground while she sat on the porch swing and shared her stories. She had lived in that neighborhood her whole life and she was in her 90's when I got to know her. I stayed overnight with her some nights as well. We chatted in the middle of the night as she would walk through the guest room where I was resting with her oxygen tubing pulled close behind as she headed to the restroom. These are memories I will never forget. She would always stop in the middle of the guest room and say, "Heather, are you awake?" It was *so* hot in her home, as she was elderly and always cold, and of course I was not able to sleep anyways because of my insomnia. Nights with Ms. P were always a hoot. The same happened in Germantown where I lived in Philly or in North Philly where I did home visits with patients living with HIV. I had so much more to learn than I had to give.

Listening at the Feet

Serving the unhoused at the Open Door Community in Atlanta, was another deeply heart-shaping opportunity. I went there during nursing school at times to help serve breakfast. But it seemed that the biggest complaint I heard from our unhoused friends was that their feet hurt. So for my senior project, I started a foot clinic there along with my close friend Joanna. We named it the Sole (soul) Care Clinic and we went every other Thursday night. One guy whose feet I was working on had walked there from jail one Thursday evening. He taught me over the course of an hour of working on his ingrown toenails and painful corns, that I should not give him or other unhoused people money. He told me what he would use it for. He said it was better to help and show love in other ways. My dad's company donated boots for each person we saw and we gave a fresh pair of socks with them, too. There was such delight in seeing what my friend from college would call "Bickel Boots" on the feet of the unhoused throughout downtown Atlanta.

Speaking of "Bickel Boots," I realize that my desire to sit at the feet of people and listen has been shaped by my dad and what he did in his career. His job was a shoe/boot salesman (he was the top salesman of his company) and his territory was the whole Southeast of the US. He would literally sit at the feet of people and listen every single day as he served his customers, and they loved him. He worked hard and he provided well for us by working so hard. He even provided *all* that he had for this foot clinic to be successful, including hundreds of pairs of boots!

I will never forget one guy named Jerry's response after we got his toenails cut from sticking into the bottom of his toes because they had grown so long. He danced and twirled down the hallway of the shelter saying, "you have given me my wheels back." I was in tears as it really hit me that his feet were his "wheels"—his only mode of transportation.

There is so much to be learned by sitting at the feet of people and hearing their voices. Literally being lower than, down below people and listening. It is a tender (and vulnerable) place to be. It seemed without fail on a Thursday night at the Open Door Community Homeless Shelter, Joanna, I or one of our volunteers would look up and see huge tears coming out of someone's eyes. I felt so honored to hear the *souls* of these neighbors. We would hear many times that they could not remember the last time they had been touched. So having a good foot soak, having foot ailments taken care of, getting a good foot massage and a new pair of socks and boots, was a small thing to us, but to them seemed to mean the world. We were called the "foot angels," but I felt as though we were the ones receiving the gift of being entrusted with peoples' hearts and stories as we sat at their feet.

This deep learning happened again when we moved into a predominantly Latine neighborhood in San Diego. We learned quickly by sitting under the big tree outside of our house at a busy corner, from a group of guys who dealt drugs there and had grown up in that neighborhood, that we were not to come inside of the outer gate of someone's property without being invited. We would sit for hours with these guys when we moved into the neighborhood. Sometimes it would be us bringing a box of donuts from the bakery down the block and them with a huge bucket of beer on ice, and we would just ask them things like, "What does it mean for us to be good neighbors here?" They often would share things like the importance of keeping the sidewalk washed in front of our house, the palm trees trimmed back, and our cars parked on the street clean. We learned that it's loving and right to linger longer with our neighbors, to not just wave from across the street, but to hang out, even if it meant being really late to wherever we thought we needed to go. It took years of listening to gain their trust and to know what was really going on in the neighborhood. We discovered the importance of being constant learners. Our neighbors became super interested in hearing our voices, too. They asked direct questions and were so curious to hear why we chose to live there. What an honor to be known there.

We felt loved more than we showed love as we got to know our new neighbors. Many of our neighbors had never had gringos in their home, so to be invited into homes and to really hear people's life stories was quite the honor. One woman, while walking past the house with her two-year-old, had just lost his sippy cup. She was on the way to the bus to head to the ER because she was having a miscarriage. Meeting her that night outside became the beginning of a now 5-year friendship. We journeyed with her as she left her domestic violence situation and fled with her kids. She is a close friend now, thriving in life and in her relationship with God. This all happened as a result of helping her look for a lost sippy cup.

So many life principles have been so slowly learned by short stints overseas like in North Africa—learning quickly not to put the bottom of my shoe to face a person. Staying there with a family who did not speak English or Spanish, I was learning how to love and learn without using words. What a challenge! It was also understood in that part of the world that if someone came to your house you would welcome them in, have tea and let them stay as long as they desired. Even if you had plans, it was never appropriate to say that you needed them to leave. I learned so much about these things from a family I stayed with that I knew from seminary who were missionaries there long term.

I was always learning and failing, learning, and failing, and constantly being stretched outside of my comfort zone. You should see my journals! My fear was ever so present, and I was humbled and dependent on God to use my shaky voice. I was seeking to be a good neighbor and friend and seeking to love well. Most of this has been formed in me through being in relationship with my dear soul mate, Jeremy and doing life alongside him. We have learned the most through failing quite a lot and learning from our mistakes.

Listening to the Heart

When I was a nurse in Atlanta at a clinic that predominantly served immigrants from Mexico, I heard border crossing stories almost daily and was told often by my patients "the US wants our hands for work but not the rest of us. It doesn't seem this country wants our families, to care for our bodies, or to help us when we are sick." I was in tears most days. This had not been something I had learned much about growing up. There were many times I just found myself apologizing for what people were experiencing as immigrants in this country. I loved doing adult primary care at this clinic in South Atlanta and we ran a prenatal program as well. The clinic services were for people who either were not US citizens or for those who could not afford health care in other places, and we functioned on a sliding-fee scale program based on people's word.

Sometimes we would see over 45 pregnant women in an afternoon. Those were my favorite days that happened about once a week. On the other days, it was mainly adult medicine. It was no normal clinic though. On some days it was like a miniature ER. I saw one man that walked in after just being shot. We had people coming in having a heart attack, with big wounds, or in labor. We honestly never knew what would happen in a day. I sure loved my co-workers.

I remember this one dear man who came in over and over for his allergies. He was miserable with all the pollen in Georgia. He also came in one day saying that he had something stuck in his ear. He told me what it was in Spanish, but I thought I was not understanding him. Upon looking, I was sad to see that it was a roach. It was super common for many people to sleep on the floor of a one-bedroom apartment and work 12-hour days or nights, and they were often in Georgia without their families. They were working long hours to send money home to their loved ones.

My heart and world were broken wide open at this special little hole in the wall clinic in South Atlanta. It was a *big* day when we got to move into a clinic that we were able to build with the help of many donors. Up until that point, we had functioned in little buildings that were not made to be clinics. Our dear patients would sit in the waiting room for hours upon hours to be seen. We sought to show each patient so much love, care and respect. I had the utmost respect for my co-workers and all of the volunteers. I loved getting to know our volunteers from an organization called Mission Year. They worked so so hard alongside us, for no pay. There were some days when our volunteer OB-GYN doctors would not show up as they were delayed for good reasons like having a patient in crisis at the hospital and we would *jump* into action doing all that we could in their stead. There were very few dull moments.

I could tell you countless stories about being a nurse at this clinic. It was quite an amazing first job, and I am glad I worked there because I always wanted to work at a place that would prepare me to work in an overseas context where there would likely be no doctors nearby. I always loved the nursing aspect, but I loved even more connecting with the hearts of my patients. This is why I then went to seminary to study counseling, to really learn about connecting with people's hearts.

Nursing and counseling have both been used together to open so many doors to tend to the bodies and souls of people. In Atlanta and once we moved to San Diego, I have heard so many stories of pain either at the border, seeking to cross the border, or the awfully hard struggle once people had arrived in the States.

It was so hard not being able to speak the heart language of my patients when I first became a nurse, so I was very thankful for my volunteer translator Linda from Mission Year. That's why I spent a total of 10 weeks between Guatemala and Mexico over the years for Spanish Immersion training. I also got to use my Spanish in my work as a nurse in Georgia at the Grant Park Clinic and also at Esperanza in Philadelphia and learned how to deeply listen to people in their heart language. There is something powerful about learning one's heart language and speaking in that language, whether that be sign language (in high school), Spanish at the clinics or even charades in North Africa! In these situations, once again, I learned that the heart's desire of most is to be listened to deeply, rather than to be spoken to (it's what I have always desired for myself the most too!).

Listening to the Lessons from the Amazon

I went deep into the Amazon in Brazil when I was a brand-new nurse with a team of people. I made a lot of assumptions about what the people knew, those whom we were treating as patients. These individuals had never been given Western medicines or even seen North Americans.

My first patient had a bad ear infection. Through three translators we were able to communicate back and forth. When I gave antibiotics for the ear infection and wanted her to take the first one right then with the clean water that we brought, she immediately went to put the pill, which was to be taken orally, in her ear! I was able to stop her and explain more about taking it in her mouth to treat the ear infection, but this was a humbling learning experience and prepared me for the days to come. We would have more than 100 patients lined up daily, spanning deep into the Amazon.

I will never forget heading from the bigger boat out on a little boat on the first day of this trip. I had my stethoscope flopping around my neck and I found myself wanting to turn around and go back to the big boat. I was scared to death. I had *no* idea what I was doing or who or what (in regard to health ailments) we would see in a day. I have never prayed so much in my life.

Also, those two weeks I didn't sleep at all. It was me and one of our nursing instructors and then nine nursing students. We slept on hammocks on the boat, super close to one another. When one person would roll over on their hammock at night, we'd all have to roll over. I'd lay in the hammock, awake all night, listening to the different sounds and watch as the sun came up. I would hear the animals in the jungle and in the mornings, I could see the line of people waiting. At night, it was completely dark, there was no electricity, but I knew there were hundreds and hundreds of people out there. I was stunned as I could not see anyone, but I knew they were there. I have always been overwhelmed as I think about big groups of people and what they (and their loved ones) are facing.

When on the boat in the Amazon at night, the people could see us as we had lights on the boat, but we could not see them. I often wondered what they might be thinking of us as we did our evening things and especially during the hot afternoons when we would jump off the boat to cool off and we all knew that there were barracudas in the water. I imagine they thought we were crazy, and I sometimes think that we were.

I would lay awake all night in the hammock, and I would

think about every person we had served that day. I was thinking of those bright (and sometimes, teary) eyes that seemed to look deep into my soul. People would pull on my ears and touch my face. It was so disorienting to speak in English and have it translated to Portuguese and then into the local dialect. I was so tired every day. So scared. It changed my life. It opened my eyes to a whole level of nursing and loving people. I was so humbled, especially when I was deeply listening to people's hearts and using nursing in a way that I felt so ill-equipped for.

I was often shaking on the inside, or sometimes even on the outside! I was so nervous. It made me dependent on God and others. I found myself asking God, "Why did you bring me here? I'm leading a team and I just passed my nursing boards three weeks ago! I am not ready for this!" The nursing mentor believed in us and would remind us that we did have what it took and that we were there for a reason. God was using us. Her voice was very powerful and empowering as we faced each day. We were sometimes in a village for 17 hours. There was no going anywhere to rest. The exhaustion was profound. It was hard and amazing.

Discerning when it's best to listen or when it's best to speak and use our voice for good and when it's best not to speak is crucial to this life and to relationships with others. Sometimes I feel what I have experienced seems so trivial when compared to others lives that I have journeyed with. I have to believe that all of the opportunities God places in our lives, whether seemingly small or rather big, are all preparing us for what's ahead. Learning this lesson would prepare me for what was ahead, that was for sure! I would have never guessed or imagined what my upcoming job would be, but learning when to speak and when to listen were essential for it!

CHAPTER 7

WHEN VIOLENCE
SILENCES VOICE

ONE OF MY MANY JOBS HAS BEEN to be a coach that comes alongside women in what they are desiring clarity in or help with. Listening deeply is one of the most important skills in this role. Some of the women I have coached are in domestic violence situations. These brave souls are often told verbally and/or by other manipulative actions, "I don't want to hear your voice," "you are too much," "it's all your fault," etc. I've spent many years helping women find their voice within this situation. In coaching, counseling, nursing, spiritual direction, it all comes into play with deeply entering in to hear stories, and these stories have broken my heart wide open. How could the one person that has vowed to love you no matter what seek to intentionally do you harm?

I still feel so ill-equipped to journey with women in this situation, and it is so much more prevalent than is known. I did coaching alongside Leslie Vernick in a group of women that as of 2023 consisted of just under 3,000 women of faith. Leslie Vernick is a woman who loves God and loves God's word and has written many books on destructive relationships and marriages, as well as domestic violence. She is a speaker as well and she is well respected among churches all over the world. Many in her group are wives of pastors, elders and deacons of their local churches. If you are reading this and think "not my church," I promise you that you are wrong (please check out any of Leslie Vernick's books/ online resources for more information or if you personally need help in this area: https://leslievernick.com). Although I have not experienced domestic violence personally in a marriage situation, I have seen it up close with friends and family and have experienced the very confusing manipulation and emotional crazy-making from people I dated and also from an extended family member. More on that later.

Abuse Takes Many Forms

I will never forget riding in the car with a couple that I love so deeply! I was in the back seat and the husband and wife were in the front seat. The wife began eagerly telling a story and was in the middle of her story when, in the rear-view mirror, I saw her husband put his finger across his mouth as a symbol to the wife to stop talking, and she did. I was heartbroken and shocked. I thought, I never ever want to be in a marriage where my voice is not welcome, or even worse, silenced. It keeps me up at night to know of the sheer number of women, even within the church, and sometimes especially in the church, where voices are not welcomed or are even subtly or harshly shut down. I am in tears as I write this. Tears of sadness and anger, too.

I will never forget talking with one woman whom I was coaching, whose voice I could barely hear, as she was speaking in a hushed tone from the closet as her husband was not too far off with a gun. Other women tell me time after time that the emotional and verbal abuse and crazy-making (this is a form of psychological manipulation where someone is presented with a lose-lose situation and criticized for whichever choice they make) feels so torturous and is not seen by others, that they *wish* that their husbands would hit them just so that they would be believed.

My deepest desire is that each woman would feel seen, known, heard, loved and understood, believed, and that they would find their voice in these situations and have the courage to use it. I desire that each woman would know that the abuse is not their fault, that they do not deserve it no matter what, and that there is help (I do know that some men are the ones being abused in the relationship. I am just sharing my experience which has been journeying alongside women).

I've taken two courses and an in-depth training with Leslie's team. I learned that abuse could take so many forms: verbal, emotional, financial, physical, sexual, etc. With three of my closest friends, it's emotional, verbal, neglecting, and crazy-making. They tell me often how much they wished they would be punched so that it would be so much easier than things like having their car keys hidden or being made to feel like they are crazy and that all the conflict and issues are their fault. They walk on eggshells in their own homes.

I did experience some hints of crazy-making, manipulation and verbal abuse in my own dating relationships. It was just a small, small taste of what my friends and coaching clients have been living in for years on end. Some friends were dating narcissists and didn't know. For some, within three days of marriage, their spouses checked out. For others, their husbands have been found to be completely addicted to pornography.

I had the opportunity to use my voice to speak about domestic violence and to teach about it to our community health promoters when I worked at Esperanza Health Center in North Philadelphia. There are things in this life, such as this horrid experience, that I hope I will *never* shy away from entering into with my voice.

One memory lodged in my mind, which happened shortly after going through one of my first domestic violence training sessions, happened while I was out on a walk in my neighborhood and a young gal ran up to me crying, shaking and with some cuts on her arm. She said that she had just been raped and needed help. We called her parents, and she did not want me to call the police. I got her to a safe place off of that street while we waited for her parents. I communicated to her that this was not her fault, she did not deserve that for any reason and that there was help. As she told her story to her parents, I encouraged her to report this to the police. She was so scared. I had given her and her parents my cell number in case they needed it. I went home and wrote down as many details as I could remember that she told me.

Months later I got a call from her attorney, and she asked for my version of the story. I had no idea that this young brave gal had indeed reported it. I told the attorney my version of what she had told me and then I was told when I needed to appear in court. The attorney mentioned something about an expert witness, and I said, "oh, I am glad there will be an expert witness," and she said, "yes, that expert witness is *you!*" Oh, my word! I began to shake. I was thankful that the day court happened, the guy who raped her pled guilty before we went before the judge because he found out she had an "expert witness." It was a relief and a wakeup call that we can use our voice in powerful ways.

Being Silenced in Relationships

When so much of my worth comes from the opinion of others, words can be so powerful. As a freshman in college, my roommate told me I was "the ugliest person" she "had ever seen." This echoed what another family member had said when I was in Middle School along with what I felt was true of me throughout my growing up years. I had trouble feeling accepted as I was. I was also in a good

86

number of dating relationships from high school and a couple in college and then some after college. Several men that I dated said that God told them that I was supposed to marry them. I responded that "God did not tell me the same thing." This went on up until I was 35 and finally started to date my husband-to-be, Jeremy.

One thing that meant so much is a couple guys I had dated had strong boundaries physically, and they held to them. That really meant a lot to me. I also spent a lot of time in dating relationships super confused, especially right after I became a Christian in college. To be pursued, to know that others really approved of the relationship, and to be told I was loved, I just kind of put aside any questions I truly had deep in my heart. I was also super unsure of myself, did not listen to my own gut, and was super swayed by others' opinions. This made being clear and honest with God, myself and these guys quite difficult. I often doubted my own heart and the unrest that was deep within me, so I know that this was not easy for the guys I dated either. There are many times I wish I could go back and apologize for my own confusing messages that I gave.

In reading through my old journals, I can see in hindsight that me not trusting my own voice, and putting more weight into the person I was dating, was swaying me into believing they were right and that I was probably wrong. Had I taken the time to listen deeply to my heart, I would not have led guys on in our relationship, or been as confusing, but would have ended things much more quickly.

One of the hardest things that I faced consistently in each dating relationship was that marriage was brought up within the first month to three months of dating. This felt like so much pressure and that I could not enjoy just dating and getting to know someone. I was often journaling about "is this the one I am supposed to marry?" It felt like torture and so confusing, as their confidence in the, "yes, we are to be married," was never the same way I was feeling or sensing God leading (well, until Jer. Then I knew within a *week*! More on that later).

87

Back to the complexity of dating. I knew I was swayed by their opinions and confidence in how God was "speaking to them," and for that, I was super confused and would say or do things I was not ready to say or do. Then, there are other dating situations in which I wish I could go back and say to some guys, "*What were you thinking*?!" Sometimes it was over-the-top pursuit (in college having a boyfriend make copies of my senior picture and blow it up and put it on every car window, classroom door, dorm room door and the student center on my birthday). I hated being the center of attention and was mortified. It was love-bombing and it was not appropriate.

Other times dating was downright confusing and inconsistent. Some other examples of going over-the-top, post my college years, were things like being walked into a ring store when I was nowhere near ready to get engaged and had clearly said so. When I realized he was not going to let me leave the store until I pointed at something, I sheepishly and very reluctantly pointed out the smallest ring I could find to just get it over with. Having a small ring is me, but he promptly said, "no, I will get you the biggest ring I can find." He truly was not listening to me or respecting me at all. His plans were not considerate of me, but only what he wanted, when he wanted it, and I was not going along with his master plan. The size of the ring was all about him being able to show it off. He also requested I wear my hair down more and wear skirts. He voiced being ashamed of me when I said in front of his prestigious friends, "sleep good," instead of "sleep well." Never have I made that mistake again. *Ugh.*

Then there were times when someone did sidewalk chalk messages covering my parents driveway overnight, or wrote a song that was performed in front of others, when my least favorite thing is being put in the spotlight! I was also asked early on in relationships how I would feel about being a pastor's wife or a doctor's wife. I was told in one relationship we would get married, he would pursue his career, and I would stay home and raise kids. Things had always been just as he had planned, and so me pushing up against that and saying "no" was not welcomed at all. Thankfully my female friends and mentors were quick to speak into this.

My voice was often not heard, especially my, "no." I had one guy I was dating share his struggles with pornography with me quite often, while at the same time telling me that I was just not the "supermodel" he was looking for to marry. This same man would not even give me a side hug, but would look at porn instead? It just was so confusing. I thought, if this is what a relationship with a godly man looks like, I think I will stay single! It seemed in some relationships all that was wanted was to have all of my attention and to have physical affection, but then there were a couple guys who said they would not touch me until we were married.

One of the mothers of a guy I had dated told me that if I could not keep a perfect house or make the meals she had made for her son, then I "clearly was not the one for him!" This was an extremely hard thing to hear, not only because I was sure I could not fill those shoes, but also because it put into words what I thought about marriage and, more so, what my role as a wife would be.

Growing up in the South, I had thought that my role as a wife was to: 1) submit to my husband and fulfill his desires, 2) to keep a tidy home, decorate, cook and care for the kids, 3) to put my needs last. These things were ingrained in me through my own family, through church, through watching other marriages of friends that got married soon after college, etc. The scary thing was, I knew I couldn't do any of that, nor did I really desire to. Uh oh, what did this mean?

So, in other relationships, guys would push through physical boundaries I had set or that we had agreed upon. There were a couple godly men that I dated that faithfully showed me what the love of God and a relationship of grace could look like. Sadly, one of them had been ready to propose for a bit and was waiting patiently for me, then when I finally said I was ready, he promptly broke up with me. This happened back and forth with him 4 times! He would come back saying "he just *knew*" we were supposed to get married and then the next day he would "lose peace again." One day, while we were still together, he was playing violin outside of my room in Philly where all eight of my roommates could hear and he had just been talking about flying to ask my dad for my hand in marriage, and days later, he broke up with me. He said, "I expect to have unwavering passionate feelings for the person I will marry, and I don't have that." As soon as I moved from Philly to date someone else, he told my mentor he made a mistake and knew he was supposed to be with me. When I moved back to Philly, he knew that he was not supposed to be with me. He soon got engaged to someone else. *Ugh.*

Literal quotes from my journal of things guys said to me were: "you have commitment issues" and "you are just not listening to God." One said, "get over your anxiety and just kiss me." I can honestly say that I got to the point where I was so content with being single that I truly thought that I would be single for life. After having so many hard/confusing dating experiences and then seeing how difficult so many marriages were around me, I was really at peace with being single.

So although I have not been in a marriage that is destructive, I have been in dating relationships where I knew, deep down, for a *long* time that I needed to get out, that they were not healthy for me. In reading whole journals full of my wrestlings in these relationships, my trying to end things and not being able to, it's the smallest taste of what some of the women I meet with experience every day. They think, "Why can't I get out?" "What is wrong with me?" "Did I cause this or deserve this?" "Is what he says about me really true?" "I am so messed up, if I would just do what he says maybe things would be more peaceful." I felt crazy in some of these relationships. How could I have "commitment issues" like some guys said, when I had been a bridesmaid in dozens of weddings? If anything, I was *over*committed!

Through each of these dating examples, I do not believe anything was wasted. I was shaped and formed to become the woman, friend and counselor that I am today. I see clearly that I could've done things so differently had I known my own heart and voice better. The voices and opinions of others and my own fear of rejection played a big role in my relationships and the decisions that I made in them. I really do take full responsibility for my actions, and I believe that many of these men sought to love and show care the best that they knew how at that time, and for that I am thankful.

The things that people say get so lodged in our soul, especially the negative things. So many lies that can keep us *stuck* in something that is not God's very best for us. I am so thankful that I had godly women around me that would reflect back my voice. In reading my journals from those seasons now, I can see why I was so drawn to be a coach for women in destructive relationships or marriages. I can say to women in relationships that are destructive in any way, that there is help, it's *not* your fault and you do not deserve this if you are in a relationship like I have described above. I hope you can find your voice too and be able to walk in freedom. There is *so* much more and *better* on the other side.

The Complexities of Dating and Finding Your Voice

The man that I dated before beginning to date my dear Jer, was a man that God truly used to show me the kindness, patience, and the humility of Jesus. It was so odd when my heart just shut down towards him and I honestly told him, "At this point, I really do not think I will ever get married." The times that I broke up with some of these good, dear and godly men left my heart absolutely crushed and feeling absolutely terrible. Sometimes I thought to myself, "Heather, what is wrong with you?" and others in my life asked me the same question. But, with other relationships, when we broke up, I felt like I had been set *free*!

When I approached my early-to-mid 30's and was still single, older people in my parent's church would ask me things like "Do you even like guys? How are you 35 and single?" or "Why don't you have kids? Do you not like them? You are so selfish!" or "Must be nice that you get to do whatever you want to do, and not have to answer to anyone." Words also have been given that are such pat answers—"God is sovereign over your suffering." "If you are content in your singleness, that is when God will bring your husband." "The saying is true about you, Heather, 'always a bridesmaid, never a bride.'"

I was so incredibly thankful that one day I prayed that God would open a man's heart towards me and my heart towards that man at the *same* time, and the very next day after writing that prayer in my journal when I was 35 years old in August of 2011, God did that with my husband-to-be, Jeremy and me at the same time! Literally, on the exact same day, God opened up our hearts wide open to each other.

I did have to use my voice in our dating months because we got engaged so quickly and after we did, we quickly began preparing for our wedding that was originally going to be on New Year's Day, 2012. Jer shared some things he needed to work through in order to be able to say that wholehearted "Yes" to marrying me. With my past relationship experiences and knowing that it would be good for him to have whatever time he needed, we sought counsel and decided to get unengaged and call off our planned wedding date. This was a *hard* time to have to speak up because I feared that I could lose him or that there could be a "lack of peace" in him and that my heart would be broken. But I wanted nothing less than for him to feel total freedom from God in his own heart to marry me.

He worked through things quickly and was ready to get engaged again (we never broke up during this time, nor did his desire towards me ever waver), but I was simply not ready. I needed to face my own fears at that point. I needed to make sure that he was here to stay. It was around seven months later when I *proposed to him*! We had decided that when I felt ready that I would propose and that was such an amazing day. This was one of the most joy-filled moments of using my voice that came directly from my heart (Side note: I can't believe guys have to go through all those *nerves* when getting ready to propose. I was 99.9% sure he would say "yes," but my body was still shaking uncontrollably)! It was then six weeks later that we got married. Using my voice in that situation was *hard*, yet I found that Jer showed nothing but deep honor, respect, patience and understanding. I thought it was super *brave* of him to speak up in the first place that he had some things to work through.

We sure enjoyed those extra months of dating and instead of spending that time just wedding planning, we spent it truly preparing for marriage. We used a book during this time called *4,000 Questions for Getting to Know Anyone and Everyone* by Barbara Ann Kipfer to deeply hear one another's hearts, stories, background and desires for the future. We also met with Sue Lutz for counseling and did the Prepare/Enrich assessment. All of these tools were extremely helpful, and they all set us up to have a thriving marriage. I was *so* glad that we took each of these steps, although it was *not* easy to take off that ring, tell *tons* of people our wedding was off and trust God with our hearts in such a deep way. It turned out to be the very best decision we could make for our well-being and for building a solid foundation for our marriage.

I could write a whole book about this love that we share and how 10-plus years into marriage, neither of our hearts have wavered and it gets better and better every day. I am so in love with this man and feel it's the biggest privilege of my life to spend each day loving him and being loved by him. We love to invest in and love others together, too. I could not be more thankful for my dear husband, Jer.

The stark difference between many of my dating experiences compared to the privilege of dating and being married to Jer has me on my knees with thankfulness. I have seen first-hand what life could have turned out to be had I not married him, just by journeying with other ladies who live such hard lives day in and day out. We all have our own version of hard, and God placed this selfless servant-hearted man in my life for so many reasons, one of which was to help me walk through *long* seasons of illness.

CHAPTER 8

THE SIGNIFICANCE OF VOICE IN SUFFERING

I HAVE ALSO FOUND MANY OPPORTUNITIES to use my voice for others who are suffering medically, whether it be physically or mentally, and this includes my own illnesses. Unseen illnesses are awful. I experienced not being believed that I was sick for several years until my diagnoses. I can't tell you the number of times that I have had to be my own health advocate! I have not been believed by most healthcare providers throughout my journey with chronic illness. This increases the suffering more than words can express.

Even when I had severe symptoms from Lyme disease and wasn't yet diagnosed, I was just told that I was anxious or working too much. I have had so many stories of other people reaching out online that have experienced the same thing. Whenever I have shared about Lyme, multiple concussions, chronic fatigue, POTS, insomnia, depression, and more, many others can share the feeling of being unseen and unheard as they are crying out for help! Why would we make this up?

Can Illness be a Symptom of Something Deeper?

As I am writing this book, I am reading Gabor Mate's book, *The Myth of Normal*, and just beginning to wonder how much of the illnesses that I have dealt with for over half of my life have been worsened or impacted by my not being in tune with my own needs, much less honoring those needs. I have been following the journey of so many other chronically ill people, and most of us are women who have been people helpers or who have otherwise given our lives to invest in others. It could be investing in children, friends, or caregiving, etc.

It's not that it is bad to invest in others, but when we do it to the detriment of our own wellbeing, could that be a contributing factor or something that worsens the course of our illness? Sometimes we think loving others means suppressing our own voice, needs, and desires. Dr. Mate's work really talks about how this tendency can lead to physical illness. I have put my needs aside with my words and actions, and sometimes wonder how this tendency (that I have lived with since I was a young girl, and it only got more severe in my adult years) has contributed to my being ill for so long.

As I learn how to honor my voice and use it to speak my true needs and boundaries (and then keep those boundaries no matter what others think), I have become so much healthier physically, mentally, emotionally, relationally and spiritually. I have seen my body and my immune system get much stronger *even since I began writing this book.* Finding my voice, writing my voice, and honoring it, I am beginning to feel better. How fascinating, right? I do not think that the symptoms from my Lyme disease (which came from a tick bite), head injury, and years of insomnia that began at the time of my head injury are solely from not honoring my own needs. I just wonder if neglecting those needs has made it worse!?

Helping the Helpers

Why is it so hard for "helpers" to receive help? With developing postural orthostatic tachycardia syndrome (POTS) in early 2020, my body went into the most severe fight-or-flight response that I had to stop completely and not help others in the time when the whole world was shutting down with the pandemic. I am so thankful for the support of having had years of study of the nervous system through Organic Intelligence, led by Steven Hoskinson (who lives and works in San Diego with an international team). It has become such a help in realizing that I have over-functioned ever since my head injury and have sought so hard to not let any of my illnesses become my identity.

Organic Intelligence (OI) is a training that helps people understand and learn how to regulate their own nervous systems and help others do the same. My body had been screaming for rest since my head injury in 1994, but I did not listen. My friends at OI and other friends kept telling me to lean in and listen to what my body was longing for. There were so many other things that seemed so urgent for me to do. Some well-meaning people told me, "You can rest and sleep in heaven. We have work to do here." The rest, the deep rest my body so deeply needed, was now being forced on me. It was forced on me during a bout of depression while living in community in Philly and again during the pandemic when the whole world was forced to not "go and do," but to just "be." This seemed to be the hardest but most needed lesson of my life!

During these hard dark days of the pandemic, when most people felt so far away, the gift was that I got to share the day 24/7 with my dear husband, Jer. This is when he began to work from home because of the global shut down. We found new rhythms of seeking to care for one another and for our neighbors. I was so sick I could barely leave my home and couldn't drive. I felt trapped inside of my body, inside my home, and inside of my head that constantly had the voice of an inner critic saying that I had messed everything up. I was so unsure during this time if I was going to make it—if I was going to survive.

Many nights were spent in tears, curled up in Jer's arms, hearing him speak words of truth, love and comfort. There is no one else on this planet I would rather be quarantined with than this amazing man. I was told by doctors that getting Covid could kill me, so I literally did not spend time in another person's presence outside of Jer for a few years. This, as a helper, which is someone who always wants to support others, was something that I could have never imagined surviving if someone would have told me that this was going to happen. We did end up avoiding getting Covid, and we drew very close to God and to each other.

Again, my world became small, with only sending voice memos to a very small handful of women. I faced the deepest, darkest parts of myself during the days in which I sometimes felt I would not survive, or during days that I did not want to survive. I didn't even have the strength for live calls. I felt utterly helpless and useless.

I distinctly remember a season during the pandemic when Jer and I were living at a campground in an RV (*what an adventure and challenge that was!*). I was so so sick and had not seen a single friend. My dear soul sister, Lara flew from Indiana to San Diego, then drove another hour out to the RV to have a brief visit with me. I wept the minute she entered our rig (that Jer's cousins so graciously let us borrow), and I fell into her arms and hugged her as if my life depended on it.

Lara is an RN and midwife and so she even removed the IV from my arm, so that the mean home health nurse didn't need to come back. She helped us sell things on facebook marketplace from our home and has initiated and overseen several GoFundMe pages for my health expenses over the years. We have worked together, spent hours upon hours in Philly and San Diego together and have supported each other through some of the deepest of losses and grief. She has taught me so much about how to be real with my voice and to not apologize for it, ever. She stands boldly for issues of injustice and has taught me so much about these profound injustices throughout the nation and world. She and her husband, Chris, truly challenge me. They were part of starting The Simple Way community with Shane Claiborne in Philadelphia (check it out if you don't know about it: www.thesimpleway.org), and Lara and Chris continue to give their lives to fighting injustices in all areas of life. I respect them so much and am so thankful for this consistent and faithful friendship.

I have had a Caring Bridge (a free online website) to share about my illnesses and to update loved ones on my health and our lives. This has been alongside the GoFundMe pages that were started by close friends. With not being able to work and with countless medical bills being through the roof, it was necessary to ask for help from others. The Caring Bridge was super helpful to answer questions and to also share what is helpful and what isn't helpful when someone is chronically ill. When I was so sick that I could barely get out of bed, to be asked "How are you? Feeling better yet?" sometimes felt maddening. Some family members have told me that I shouldn't put my struggles out there or ask others for money, but it was necessary. It's not as if I enjoyed putting my struggles out there for all to read. As a chronically ill person and talking with others that are ill, we all want to be just believed, loved and accepted where we are. These are our biggests desires.

We have to be our own advocates—all insurance, meds, doctor notes, and follow through has all been left up to Jer and me. It seems like it was even more up to me once people found out I was a nurse. I desperately wanted someone else to be my nurse and caregiver! It was so hard to do all of this when I could barely even get to the bathroom. Many times, I wished that my health providers were unaware that I was a nurse so that I could just be a patient for a season. But that did not happen.

It was not until late fall of 2022 that I began to experience life again, more freedom, and a radical honesty with God. Jer and these few close ladies were the only ones to know what was happening inside of me throughout this whole dark season of illness. It was as if everything I had placed my hope and identity in was stripped away, and I was staring at my broken heart and body. As I looked in the mirror that fall and could see every bone from the outside with my body weighing literally in the 80's, I was shaken awake to fight! To fight hard.

In December of 2022, a big turning point came that I did not expect. A loved family member became sick and needed my care. In the process of serving and loving her, my focus shifted off myself and my own brokenness and pain, and I entered into her world and life. I began to drive for the first time in a couple of years, prayed more than I ever have, and I saw how resilient my body was, even in the midst of still being very sick. I was thankful for this time that seemed to break me out of a sort of rut and even fear of what the doctors had said, that "COVID could kill me."

When I finally got COVID at the very end of December 2022, due to a trip to the ER for something else, it did not kill me. I remember that late night in the ER, realizing that I was surrounded by people with COVID, that I could be still, peaceful and prayerful for the nurses, staff and patients around me, while realizing that soon I would surely catch COVID from there. When Jer and I both had it, we cared for one another. At that point we were living in our 13th place in two years and preparing to move yet again.

Feeling is Healing

The pandemic was a long, hard, dark winter for my mind, body, and soul. Fear, angst, illness, insomnia, anxiety, pain, and countless physical symptoms plagued my entire being. I have never fought so hard to just live and survive each day. We faced so much loss in every area of life and it began with needing to leave our beloved home and neighborhood in San Diego. In some ways it was a relief. I felt trapped, too weak to leave the house. The noise of the neighborhood overwhelmed my senses. There was nowhere to go to express myself out loud. Our house was surrounded by people, music, loud low-riders, dogs barking non-stop, etc. We had to move because my body was not doing well in our own home, which we discovered because we spent 24/7 indoors! To move quickly during a global pandemic and not having any help was plain nuts!

We moved for the first time in the pandemic just before Thanksgiving into a hotel. I fought each day to find the light in my soul and would come back to peace as often as I could. I sought to accept reality, instead of fighting against it. Our cat passed which seemed big but then I had two close girl friends pass and that was devastating, especially to not be allowed to go to their funerals because of my own fragile health. One of my very best friends got married and I had to say "no" to being her Matron of Honor. Heartbreaking! I did not have the strength to even continue doing Zoom with our families or any friends. The isolation was severe.

I sought to put the love, attention, and gentle care that I had given to others towards my own body and soul, but constantly failed at this and felt discouraged. I felt powerless and out of control. The fatigue meant Jer often needed to bring me things in bed. Going up and down the steps of the hotel was like climbing a mountain. Nurses came to give me IVs at the hotel. The first nurse that came hung the fluids on the pole incorrectly and also left me alone with the IV in my arm. Consequently, the IV pole almost fell on my head and I also had to take the IV out of my right arm by myself.

Having to speak up to managers at the home health agency was a whole new and challenging experience. Melt downs became a daily occurrence and I used my voice to let Jer and a couple close lady friends into the mess and brokenness. The taskmaster inside of my head constantly told me I was failing—failing Jer, our families, and everyone. My voice seemed to not matter at all or register with my doctors no matter how hard I tried to describe what was going on with my body. Most of them seemed to not care and were tired and overwhelmed anyways. I had 18 doctors! Insurance was making huge mistakes with billing and the main hospital where my virtual care was taking place was hacked and I had no access to my doctors for a season. Doctors called in the wrong meds, and I was given other meds that made my body go into a worse state of fight-or-flight with the POTS. Medical trauma is so real!

With my body having no temperature control, I constantly needed an ice hat and ice packs laid over my body. It felt as if I was running a constant marathon. Very few seemed to really care or get it. I realized that "feeling really is healing" and I began to express, with all the energy I had left, these emotions to Jer, my counselor and my few friends.

I found myself setting dates in my head about 1-2 months in the future for which I would persevere to and then if the suffering continued, I knew that I would need to do something different than I was doing. I felt such deep anger. It felt like the anger which I had not really felt the freedom to express throughout my life was *all* coming out. But Jer was the only one around and so I expressed it to him and I hated this. Why did I have to be sick since day one of my marriage to my dear Jer? I wrote in my journal and told my dear husband that I wanted to die. I was never suicidal, I just prayed God would take me.

The nights were the hardest. The hardest thing was that I didn't like me, and I looked for love from others and it just wasn't filling me up. Rock bottom. Outside of the handful of close girl friends, the people I talked with seemed to minimize what I was experiencing and comments or questions such as, "How are you," "Are you better yet," made me mad and made me feel so unseen and misunderstood. How was I supposed to honestly answer those questions? I know that this was not done by them on purpose, yet it hurt.

Thankfully Jer, a couple doctors, a few close friends, counselors, neighbors, my Organic Intelligence community and a few others were truly there and were a great support. We moved from the hotel into an AirBnB, then to a friend's house to house-sit over the holidays. Then into another studio AirBnB and then into the middle of nowhere in a trailer that we borrowed from Jer's cousin. It was a gift to be out of the city, but the dogs, noises from other rigs, the noise of the honey wagon draining our waste a couple times a week early in the morning, and the distance from anything familiar made this a weird but strangely refreshing experience. We did our taxes next to a fire pit and Jer and I had many conversations about deep things of the heart. Testing revealed I had very little blood flow to my brain, and it was almost impossible to think clearly. I lived so over-stimulated because of the sheer exhaustion of fighting for my life, that I put an autoreply on my phone for an entire year so that no alerts would come from it. I barely made any phone calls at all. The exhaustion and illness were unbearable.

Moving Toward Peace

We moved from the RV into a Casita where we had a landlord that inappropriately voiced a lot of personal struggles to us. Throughout this time, I received IVs twice a week wherever we lived. After a year living on the same property with this lady, we moved into an apartent above a garage where there was no air conditioning. It was closer to the beach, so it had a breeze. I had to use my voice to speak up to the owners who had a belief that my lack of faith was what was causing my illness—that if I really, fully *believed* God could heal me, then He would. This was hard for me because I don't agree with this way of thinking about how God works. They meant well and we had a good relationship with all our landlords, including them. After this house, we moved into a small one-bedroom apartment behind a big house in the city. This last place was our favorite move out of all our many moves. It was close to many places we could walk to and with woods and a trail behind the house that we could walk on. It was our first time having a landlord that just let us truly have space and do our own thing in the apartment we were renting behind their house.

Throughout all of these moves I was completely drained, even though Jer did practically all the moving and settling for us over and over. My blood pressure and pulse changed so drastically from laying to standing that I came close many times to losing consciousness. I was in severe pain in my gut if I laid down, but when I got up, I had no blood flow to my brain and could not think.

I had to use my voice constantly to get different home health nurses as they simply did not know how to start IVs. I was told by a new primary care doctor that "I was too complex for her caseload and that she did not have time to see me." Thankfully, I switched hospitals and got a great PCP that took excellent care of me. A sleep study happened on the day before Christmas Eve and there was a test where I had to swallow a pill to see why my digestion was not working. I did find joy in seeking to be kind to each health care worker I met during all of this hard testing and sought to encourage them in their job. I was so so thankful that my close friends had started a GoFundMe to help us with medical bills and living expenses. This felt humbling but I communicated my gratitude to them in any ways that I could. I am thankful for every penny that people donated to us. It encouraged my faith and my soul.

The New Me

In my journal during this time, I wrote that for 45 years I had been who people needed me to be. I didn't know who I truly was or what I really wanted. In hitting rock bottom, I began to explore this more deeply, to see the traumas for what they were, and became radically honest with myself. With having so much neuro inflammation, it was so hard to even have the most basic of thoughts. I wanted to trust that I was right where I was supposed to be, yet I was fighting it with all that I was. I knew there was no going back to living every day at 100 miles per hour. Those days were done. A new me was forming.

I let go of my lists of things to do, let go of hoping/expecting people to respond, and released doctors from "getting it" or having answers to what was happening in my body. I began to go slow and deeply listen to my own voice and the quiet voice of God. I sought to let go of seeking to manage how others saw me. I began to speak up more often to others when I felt hurt. I honored my very small bandwidth for life each day. I let go of what others thought about the auto reply on the texts on my phone. I began to walk more in line with my heart's desire that God placed within me, instead of just the "should's" and "ought to's." I started to really believe that I should "go where I was celebrated not just tolerated." People that I reached out to on text or Instagram or other platforms seemed to be ghosting me. *Was I a burden? Were my needs just too much?* I finally just let go. This was *huge* for me! Why would I ruminate over these relationships and keep going back for more lack of response or care. No more.

This welcome prayer, given to me by my friend Christiana, was a breath of fresh air that sustained me through many hard days. It's by Father Thomas Keating. Most days I did not have words of my own to pray for myself, so I prayed this:

Welcome, Welcome, Welcome.
I welcome everything that comes to me today, because I know it's for my healing.
I welcome all thoughts, feelings, emotions, persons, situations and conditions.

I let go of my desire for power or control.
I let go of my desire for affection, esteem, approval and pleasure.
I let go of my desire for survival and security.
I let go of my desire to change any situation, condition, person or myself.
I open to the love and presence of God and God's actions within.
Amen.

With only being able to be out of bed for 4 hours a day at a max, one hour was taking medications, two hours were dealing with our broken medical system (in the time surrounding appointments, meds, dealing with insurance, getting IVs at home), 1 hour for trying to eat, and barely any time for anything else. This was the sum of many days during the pandemic. My world was so limited. But my learning about boundaries during this incredibly hard season of life was crucial. In implementing these boundaries and getting to know more of who I truly am and what those "holy yes's" are, it was for my own good and the good of others and helped me understand how to use my limited energy and voice for good.

Words Can Heal and Harm

Words have played both a healing role (especially by a few close, beloved friends and family members), and they have also been used as what feels like weapons to my soul. I have been told countless times that I "look great," and thus I "can't be sick." I have been told by loved ones that are mothers, "Oh, mamas don't have time to be sick." As if I was choosing this awful state of being. And most of them did not even know that I had been a mother for some weeks before a miscarriage.

At one point during the illness between 2020 and 2023 when I was under 80 pounds, at my sickest, I was told I looked great! What?! A comment from another person was "You look like you are anorexic; you need to eat this whole pound cake." It's been so hard throughout my adult years to have my weight fluctuate so radically, and to have people comment one way or the other. The comments ranged from: "You look better with more meat on your bones," to "You are way too skinny; are you eating? What is wrong with you?" to "You look fat; you are plump now, what changed?" to "Are you pregnant?"

I don't understand why anyone (even family) would feel it's okay to make comments about my or anyone else's body. It really is something that is not appropriate. When I was at my sickest with POTS, it was like my body was running a marathon every day. No matter how many times, or how much, or how often I ate each day, I could not gain weight. So to have comments come from every single person I was with, or to have people look me up and down, was humiliating. I was almost glad that there was a pandemic, such that most people could not see me!

I beg you friends, please hold your tongue if you have a comment about someone's body. Think before you speak and ask yourself "Will this really be a productive and helpful comment to this person?" I can tell you from decades of personal experience, the answer is usually, "No!"

Even being as underweight, weak, and death looking as I was, I was *still* not believed by so many doctors, family members, and friends and was told that nothing was wrong with me. Even before I was diagnosed with Lyme disease, I had been sick for so long and had seen over 20 specialists and had been told that I was fine—that I just needed to have less stress in my life (I have seen this happen with more women than men, and it's frankly just flat wrong). I began to find ways to express myself to those that did not believe me, but sometimes had to just find peace in knowing that no matter what I communicated verbally, some people would just not get it. That had to become OK. I needed to use my voice with those that did believe me, as my energy was so low. Learning

107

how to use my voice, even with family, has been quite the learning curve.

CHAPTER 9

USING VOICE WITH FAMILY

IT'S ONLY BEEN SINCE BEING MARRIED to my dear Jeremy that I have grown more confident in holding boundaries and speaking the truth to my family. In regard to my relationship with Jer, my mom had long had it in her heart and mind that we would have a large wedding in the South. She would often say to me in my 20's and 30's, "I don't want to plan your wedding from a wheelchair." I am sure she was just seeking to joke, but even those that love us deeply can make the most interesting and unknowingly-hurtful comments. When I finally got engaged, mom began contacting her florist friend and others in GA for a big wedding!

A Philly Wedding

Long story short, we ended up having a wedding in Philly in my backyard in the middle of July (on the hottest day of the longest heat wave in the last 100 years in Philly) with people sitting on blankets on the grass or in lawn chairs. We invited everyone to come casually and so our guests were dressed in shorts and T-shirts and my dear groom was comfortably in his birkenstocks. We had Chick-fil-A and BBQ catered, a friend made a huge tower of different types of cupcakes (even some gluten free ones), and it was simple and beautiful. Our backyard became the most beautiful wedding venue thanks to our hard-working family, roommates, and close friends.

We had an open invite to our family and friends, which was done through email and online platforms. No official invitations and no bridesmaids or groomsmen. It was nothing of what my parents or many others expected, but exactly what Jer and I wanted. The most peaceful and worship-filled day of my life! Mom and dad were both so happy on that day and my dear mama helped make the wedding happen in 6 short weeks! She is a master planner and had helped me throw literally between 50-75 wedding and baby showers for friends before I even got married. We love doing that together! I had never thought I would be a bride, but I'm so thankful to have been one on July 6th, 2012.

As was planned, Jer and I had our first kiss right after we were pronounced husband and wife. So, needless to say, we wanted a *short* engagement! We knew our wedding day was exactly what we wanted and whoever was supposed to be there would be there even with such short notice. I don't like it at all when people are not happy with me, so that was a struggle. We live-streamed it for anyone who couldn't be there. To have people in N. Africa, Germany and almost all the states watching online was so encouraging. I had to let go of seeking to please people. In fact, we made a good number of people upset at our short notice, but in the end it truly did not matter. My dear organizer of a hubby had spreadsheets for everything and my Philly roommates, coworkers from Esperanza and friends from all around made it happen!

Being a Parent to My Aging Parents

Throughout my life, in order to seek to be liked and keep my family happy with me, I have been overly available to friends as well as my family. I have wanted to be noticed, loved, and accepted by them. It's only been in my 40's that I have truly begun to lay down this heavy burden of being the one to "fix things," and have started asking for more help from others. This plays out by holding more boundaries with my energy and time and still seeking to love with all that I am. Finding my needed "no," even when a struggling family member or friend wants to talk in the middle of the night, has been hard! I am seeing the bigger picture. The reality is that people don't ultimately *need* me. I am just a conduit of a bigger *love* that is the true *need*.

As I write this book, I have been thrust into a whole new season of life. Learning how to be a parent to my aging parents—meal planning, clothes choices, food, getting to doctor's appointments, house projects, you name it. I'm slowly learning what it means to help give voice for my mom as she is losing her short-term memory due to dementia. Even being an RN, I feel clueless.

My care for her is filled with love. She is still able to communicate verbally, however she can communicate so much without even using words. I can see her countenance drop when something is said that bothers her or when she feels left out or confused. I see her appetite slowing down and her ability to do things decreasing. Yet, her heart for others is so big; she always offers to help. She is still a nurse and lover of people. I am so proud of her. She does not see herself as limited much at all. In this season of living near her and being with her during doctor's appointments, it's breaking my heart to see her physically here but to not have a sharp memory (like she always has had) about what has happened or is happening. She doesn't want to tell others about this, but she says that I can tell others.

111

Mom and I have at times had the same conversation over and over. Each time it's as if the prior conversation didn't even happen. There is a challenge in it each day to never say, "I just told you that" or "Don't you remember?" because those moments prior don't exist anymore in her mind.

The gift of it is that she is in the present moment alone. There is no memory of the recent past, no real sense of time, and no concern about tomorrow. Even about traumatic things this year like ER trips where she had to be taken by ambulance on a stretcher with a neck brace on, there is zero recollection for her. I guess those are good things not to remember.

I have read a lot of books, listened to YouTube videos, and am a part of a facebook group for caregivers of people with dementia/ alzhiemers, and the trajectory of this illness is usually very dire, where some people become not able to verbally communicate at all, or not able to care for their own needs. I deeply fear this stage, and I find myself wanting to ask her so many things right now while she can still share.

I *want* to hear her voice, her stories, her desires, and what she remembers of her past. I want to know my mom in all the ways that I can. I want to use my voice to others on her behalf when she has no voice or can't remember something. I feel a desire to protect her and help her know that she is safe and cared for and will continue to be no matter what comes.

Many times, in a crowd of people, she will not talk at all because she is worried she will repeat herself. This makes me so sad. I have seen her sit completely silent, staring off in the distance somewhere, even while sitting with people who are close to us— the conversation being too much, and too confusing for her brain to engage. Yet hardly anyone knows that this is our reality. She is so loved by so many, and she doesn't need to have it together to be loved. She struggles with the same things I do. The same thing that most all of us struggle with. (In case you are curious, my parents read this book and gave us their blessing to print it.)

Letting Our Mess Be Seen

It's so clear that many of us don't want to share the reality of what is going on with our own lives, whether it be mentally, emotionally, relationally, or physically. I just experienced a clear example of this with one of my parents' friends who was sharing about how she will go to her grave carrying the things that have happened to her throughout her lifetime. We are so afraid of letting our mess be seen and are also so fearful of sharing the things that others have done to hurt us or the things we have done to hurt others. Holding all of this in often takes an immense toll on our bodies and souls.

My hope in sharing so openly here is that you will find courage to share your stories too—the good, bad and ugly. You are worth it and your story will surely be used to help others, and it can be freeing to you as well! It sure is the case for me!

Even though I am not a parent, I am getting a taste of how hard being a parent is. I desire so much for my parents to make different decisions in the day-to-day or about their long term care, and yet, that is not something I am in control of. It's not my life and they are living theirs the best they know how.

I can only imagine that parents feel this way about their children—when they see their children making decisions that they just don't agree with, yet they know that their influence is limited. I have struggled in this season of wanting to control, wanting to dictate or seek to control the outcome. I have quickly realized that this is pointless and simply does not work.

Putting On My Own Oxygen Mask First

My parents (just as I) desire to be loved, cared for and listened to right where they are. I have had to release them to God and know that I am called to be a daughter. Sometimes I have tried to be not only a daughter, but also a nurse, counselor, plumber, tech person, planner, and organizer, and this flat doesn't work. Nor is my body well enough to do all of that. To ask and receive help during this time is so hard. Especially when the help doesn't show up. It's lonely and sad. I feel helpless most of the time and am just seeking to love them with all of my heart and still take care of myself and Jer.

People keep reminding me that I need to put on my own oxygen mask first before assisting them with theirs. Meaning, to take care of myself before taking care of other people. It's a much-needed reminder and easier said than done. I did get to spend a portion of time in a cabin in solitude close to my parents' house. This was so good for my soul and brought perspective to this hard situation.

Pulling away to be with God and deeply listen to His voice and my own soul cries is essential and so grounding. Not many people understand why I would do this now, not even my parents, but for me it's a great reminder that I am not the one in control, and the last thing I ever want to create with any other human is a dependence on me. We have got to reach out to God and to our communities for help, and that seems to be very hard for most of us!

I continue to wonder what makes it so hard to ask for and to receive help from others. I so wish my parents would honestly share with others what is going on with them. This load would be so much easier if it was carried by a community.

It's also been hard as my dad is not a caregiver or the "helper" type. He has been a provider my whole life, but when it comes to caregiving, that has been my mama's role! I have had to use my voice to speak some very direct words to him in this season, which I had *never ever* done previously. I have spoken up on behalf of myself and my mom and have done it with much fear and my whole body literally trembling. Thankfully, it has been well received by him. I have been so grateful for that, and it has grown my courage to speak up more often. I know that it has grown our relationship as well.

Speaking Up with Family

I find myself wondering why it can be so hard to speak up to family and especially the men in my family. What am I afraid of? Am I alone in feeling this way? I go back to the months that it took to get up the courage to speak to my male extended family member about those inappropriate interactions I shared about before and *bam*, Jeremy and I were kicked out of this person's house with nowhere to go. It was so ugly. I didn't even really have a chance to have a conversation about what was going on.

There are various family members and close friends who struggle with mental health issues or addictions (don't we all in some form or fashion?), and I find that sometimes these things are the hardest to identify and talk about. I can share my own struggles with depression or anxiety, but it seems that really going into those topics with family is super hard. I am a trained counselor and have talked with countless clients and even strangers about these hard topics, but for some reason, it's hard to talk to those closest to me.

I feel a level of concern at the gut level for others, yet there seems to be this invisible "don't ask, don't tell" rule and it's hard to break through that. Thankfully some loved ones have started to identify unresolved trauma and have begun to talk about it (not necessarily with me). I am thankful it's being identified and shared. Sometimes I can feel like: am I the only *mess* over here? I am thankful to have my own psychologist and psychiatrist in this season of life, to whom I feel thankful that I can open up with. They are helping me even navigate these specific areas of life.

The hard truths I have had to "say" to my dad, I have mostly done over email. There are things I do not want to say in front of my mom, as I don't want her to feel uncomfortable, and it's next to impossible to get time with him alone. When we are together, it's mostly small talk. It seems putting these harder truths in written words is somehow easier, and I guess it gives him a way out or time to think about it. I feel *so* uncomfortable sending those emails, and many times I am speaking things on behalf of my mom. The amazing thing is my dad has had a humble heart and has been open to what I have to say. I have deeply appreciated this, and it has increased my courage. I believe that in his heart, he wants to do what is best for my mom, he just sometimes doesn't know what to do or how to handle these challenging times. We are all doing the best we can.

Just today, I had a conversation with my mom about something he had said, and she shared her heart *so* honestly. I wish she could use her honest vulnerable voice like this with him and others. She never could do that growing up and she doesn't feel the freedom to do it now. I wish she felt more freedom to make her desires known.

It's exhausting to speak up and say the hard things, but I have seen the fruit of it even after talking to my dad, and that it matters. It's so messy and I have not done this perfectly (not even close and he and others have given me grace) but speaking up for those that can't speak for themselves and giving voice to my deep heart pain is critical. I am seeking to do it quickly as hurtful things happen so that my heart does not become bitter. I am growing!

My mom still does not want many others to know how much of her memory is gone. So many of us don't share because of embarrassment, fear of what people will think of us, or how others will treat us. Maybe her fear is that friendships will change, and people will not see her the same. People will not need her as much or call on her for help. I get it, I am wired the same.

She has been a nurse and a people-helper her whole life; the last thing she wants is to be the one that needs help. But no matter what someone is going through, we are all human and all worth being loved right where we are, right? It's just now in my 40's that I have found that I can be truly free to express my heart, needs, wants, desires, and traumas. This is not how I grew up, but it is so freeing to be gut-level honest about where I'm at. I am also discovering that as I am vulnerable with others, they feel more freedom to be vulnerable with me, too.

Weeks after writing these last paragraphs, I have spoken up to my parents about what I think the best plan is for their long-term care. Jeremy helped me as well, and they responded positively! Thankfully, even though my dad is hesitant, we are moving forward with getting them more help with mom's care.

I had a sweet and sad time with mom as I did an interview of sorts and recorded it on my phone of what her desires are for her care going forward, as well as her desires for her funeral. She was super honest with me and I could truly hear the fear underneath her words about the days to come.

Oh, how I long for the very best for my parents. I wish I knew the right questions to ask or how I could draw out more of both of my parents' stories. My dad is not one to share about himself or his life. Many times, it's one-word answers from him (he gives the best hugs though!). I long to know so much more of *their* back stories and what shaped them. I know there is a day coming soon when my mom likely will not have many (if any) words at all, and so I am seeking to make the most of the time I have, listening to her and being with her. She has given so much of her life to my dad, and my brother and I, and I want her to feel deeply safe, loved and cared for.

Family friends and people from church have told me all of the things that I "should" be doing for them and it's always more than what is humanly possible. At least for the capacity that I have. I have found my voice in speaking up about how unhelpful this

117

is to have people dictate from the outside what those "shoulds" are. I "should-on-myself" plenty! I wonder if people have things they think I should be doing, why they don't step up and do it themselves. I have sought to graciously communicate this to these well meaning souls. I am dealing with my own illnesses and am seeking to take care of myself and simply cannot be a superwoman in these overwhelming times. I want to live with no regrets, but also don't want to lose myself in the midst and wake up one day soon not being able to get out of bed again. I have been there and done that. *No* thanks!

It has hit me in this season that more is expected of me than of others, since I do not have kids. My brother Brandon lives far away and has three little ones. He is an amazing father and has an amazing wife, Lindy (my first sister!). She and my brother are both super hard workers and are two of the most respected staff within the Colorado mountain Vail Resorts. Brandon has a heavy load. I wish I got to share more of the day-to-day with him and others in our family. It's hard to want to speak up so badly to others in my parents' church and ask for help, yet my parents don't want to share. It breaks my heart to hear my parents talk on the phone or have people visit the house and hear my parents say that "everything is fine," when things are truly falling apart. I simply don't get it.

I am seeking to find what is mine to say and share, and what isn't. I have big qualms about even publishing this chapter! But this is my true voice. Why do I need to hold it together and bust my tush doing all of the things, while they are "fine." Things are *not fine*! I want to yell it from the rooftops. I want to say, *"We are drowning over here and need some help. Anyone out there?"*

Expressing Gratitude

I am thankful that I have a relationship with my family and can seek to be real with them. I am feeling the pull within me to communicate with words all of the ways that I am thankful to be a part of this family. My brother and I have always known we are wanted and loved, and we have always been provided for. We had a completely different (better and more stable) growing up years than my parents had. What will it look like to help my parents finish their lives on this earth well, knowing that they did a good job? I *know* they did their very best.

As a caregiver and empath, I am quite nervous about the months and years to come and what they hold. But I want to encourage my parents and my brother (and my extended family with whom I am not in much contact with currently) about all of the ways I feel blessed to be a Bickel, and also to my in-laws about what it's like to be a Stevenson—as their sister, daughter, and aunt, and as of this year, a great-aunt.

I am a godmother to a good handful of kiddos and have the 12 *most* amazing nieces and nephews (and one great niece) a gal could ever dream of having. Loving my friends' kids and all the kids in our family, and seeing how honestly they use their voices, has deeply shaped how I use my own voice. I have happy tears just thinking of each of them.

Jeremy and I truly have had the honor of loving many little kiddos and big kids and being loved by them. Also, from day one of meeting Jeremy's parents (even when we were just friends), I felt so loved by them. I even had Thanksgiving lunch sitting next to one of Jer's sisters back in 2007 and we had no idea one day we would be sisters! They have welcomed me into their family as if I was born into it, and I know that is not the case for so many people. I gained another set of amazing parents and three more sisters, and their amazing families, too. What a gift! I want to be more present in every moment (like my mama) and communicate verbally to each of them and to you (my friends that are reading this) just how much you are a gift to me. This is a desire for this season of my life.

This level of thankfulness for family and for the growth that

119

has happened in my life, just leads me to want to pay it forward. The risk and the hard work it requires to find and use our voice is completely worth it! I have found that finding my true authentic voice has often come through having others deeply listen to me.

CHAPTER 10

THE GIFT OF BEING HEARD

BEING MENTORED, being in counseling, receiving spiritual direction, having close girl friends, and being married to Jer have been some of the most profound experiences of feeling loved, and have been the keys to finding my voice.

One time while working in Philly as a nurse at Esperanza, I took a lunch break in my car on an extremely stressful and overwhelming day. It was a day that I had not been still for even a minute, and it seemed like every patient that day had an overwhelming crisis (one patient even had a bomb go off on the second floor of her apartment just before I had arrived). I called my spiritual director at the time, Sally, and upon hearing just how overwhelmed and exhausted I was, she offered to sit quietly and pray silently for me on the other end of the phone while I just rested and prayed for a whole hour. It was one of the biggest gifts I have ever been given. We did not share words, and yet I felt so loved and deeply refreshed.

Other sessions with her and my other four spiritual directors since then, have been such a gift. They have listened to me and have not interrupted and have helped me see the hand of God in my life, even when I could not see it at all. I have poured out the most vulnerable parts of my heart and life knowing I was not being judged or thought poorly of—only held in love. What a gift! This is also one of my most favorite things to offer to others. If you find yourself reading this saying, *I want this*, there are many groups of spiritual directors, and some cities (like San Diego) have a whole network of spiritual directors. One group that can meet with people remotely worldwide can be found at: www.graftedlife.org.

The Joy of Listening and Being Listened To in Marriage

Besides being mentored, being in counseling, in spiritual direction, and also having some of the most amazing and faithful friends, I can say that the one who has listened the most faithfully and in the hardest of moments is my dear husband. This relationship has been what has truly allowed me to find my authentic voice, to share my deepest hards and traumas, to be known, to fall apart, and to be loved at my worst. He has listened to me for hours on end, and only loved me through it. He is the main one who has inspired me to write all of this.

Having been sick since the first day of our marriage and having this dear man care for me and me not doing what I thought I would do as a wife in these 10-plus years, I can honestly say that he has been the biggest gift of my entire life! I could not cook, clean, decorate, organize, or have kids. I was so sick. There have been countless days of our 10-plus years of marriage where I could not even get out of bed. But never have I ever felt like I was less than, or a bad wife, or anything less than completely loved, delighted in and accepted as I am by my dear husband.

My physical health has left physical intimacy unpredictable and not always something I was strong enough to engage in, and

Jer was always understanding and supportive with me putting my health needs first. I mean, is that an amazing gift, or what? He has sacrificed all sense of normalcy to help and serve me over these years and I can honestly say that my life is fuller and my heart so overflowing with gratefulness for a man who is the humblest person I have ever met. He has seen me at my worst (and when I say worst, I mean he has seen worse than even my own mom saw of me even throughout my teenage years!). He has loved me through all of it and continues to do so to this very day. I can honestly say throughout the years of being sick, I have had so many years that my life has been so small, and I have just survived, but Jer has never left my side. Even post-pandemic, I never tire of being near him. I cannot believe after 36 years of waiting, God brought me through many broken relationships in order to marry my best friend.

What has this looked like practically you might think to yourself? Here are a few examples. Maybe my next book will be all about what it has been like marrying the love of my life in my mid-30s. I really could write a whole book about being married to him. Since our wedding day, we have written daily in our five-year-long One Line A Day journals and we have two journals full of our highs and lows, and we have not yet had one boring day! But for now, I will start here with a couple broad strokes.

Jer and I have lived in 20 different places in these 10 years, had so much hard, and he is the most servant-hearted and best listener I have ever met. We have been forced to move twice because of mold (both times we were given a week to move by my doctors because of my body's sensitivity to it), moved in two hours out of another place because of an emotionally toxic living situation, and we moved 14 times during the pandemic. We have even lived for a period of time on opposite coasts of the country from each other in order to care for loved ones. He is a daily living picture of the heart of God.

We have lived with up to eight roommates and have lived

with skunks under one apartment that sprayed nightly, and they were eventually cemented under our apartment while we were out of town, left to die by our slumlord. Can you imagine the smell of decaying skunks? And I was pregnant! It was horrific and sad. We also had swarms of termites in that place that would land everywhere including on our bed! It's been a wild adventure, but daily we look to find something to laugh at, and we have the utmost respect for one another. To be honest, I have always had deep-trusting friendships with women, but never did I expect I could be married to a man this amazing.

In reading back through these One Line A Day journals that we have written in daily, some of the themes in these journals that stood out to me as ways he has drawn out my voice are: being quick to say "sorry," always encouraging me to pursue female friendships, never interrupting, long chats at our favorite cafes, his full support in me pursuing my dreams—even when that has meant traveling for extended periods of time for my job, his consistent servant- and kind-hearted nature that makes it safe to speak, leading solitude retreats together, walks and hikes to get to connect and chat, and reading the Bible and other books together and listening to God and one-another deeply. Also, he has created a safe space for my voice by never getting angry, listening so well, sticking by my side through all of the physical illnesses and my bouts with depression/anxiety and insomnia. He has always sought to hear my full perspective in making decisions, big or small—even when we decided to do a short vision trip to Bogota, Colombia and discerned together we were not to return long term. He has never doubted me about my illnesses, nor made little of them, but instead cared deeply for me in the midst of the pain. There is so much more, but in this relationship and because of his love and God's love through him, my voice has felt the freedom to come out of hiding!

Getting to invite other people into our home and lives together and listen deeply to family and friends as we are side-by-side, has been one of the biggest gifts. I could share so much more. Neither of us are perfect, but our key phrase in marriage has been "workin' it out" (Thank you Margaret for teaching us this phrase). We are super quick to deal with anything that comes up between us, we always have each other's backs, we have complete trust in one another, and we never talk poorly about the other. Those things have been true of our whole marriage. We are so thankful for each other and our families and close friends who have been by our side through some super tough years.

Regardless of your relationship status, whether you're single, married, divorced, or widowed, you are valuable, and your voice needs to be heard. Before I met Jer, I relied on God and close friends to be that listening ear for me. At other times, it was a counselor, spiritual director, or mentor. Even when there's nobody else around, you can listen to yourself or journal your thoughts. I want you to remember, you are not alone. Don't let fear hold you back from experiencing the gift of being heard.

CHAPTER 11

LISTENING IN SOLITUDE

DURING COLLEGE I WENT on retreats to listen to God's voice and the still, small voice inside. These were transformative experiences for me as I was developing my voice and identity. I have done this on my own after college by staying for a weekend at a time in a monastery in Georgia. Then when I moved to Philly, there were hermitages outside of Philly and I would go for a weekend of solitude there about once a quarter. In San Diego, I have done solitude retreats on my own and we have led groups at our friends' house in Julian, CA.

In these times in group solitude, we offer optional times for the guests to come together for a reading of scripture or some other writing to help us draw near to God and hear His still, small voice. I saw such value in doing solitude retreats myself, that getting to lead groups in Georgia, Philly, and San Diego has been such a delight. We love to prepare a space for others to turn off their phones, and to provide meals and resources or ideas for how to structure the time.

It has been a *true* joy to have people join us for their very first solitude retreat or to return again and again. Sometimes it has been just me and one or two other women, other times there were up to ten of us that went to be in solitude together. It might seem strange to think about having meals together and not talking, but each time I have done this, the food has taken on a whole new level of taste and there is a deep freedom in not *having* to talk. To continue in quiet, while in the presence of others, is a true gift. I have joked with my mentors that had it not been for Jeremy, I think I could have been a nun!

When Jeremy and I were dating and engaged, we would go once a month for a weekend to a retreat center outside of Philly where Jer studied spiritual formation and I studied spiritual direction. It's wild because when people asked me if I would ever lead solitude retreats for guys, I would say, "Well, if I get married one day, hopefully my husband will desire this as well!" Sure enough, soon after Jeremy and I got married, he was eager to lead retreats. We have both led these retreats together in Philly and in San Diego for both men and women. What a blast!

California Dreams

Our dream now is to create a place in Southern California, where people can pull away from the noise in our world, from the fast pace and all of the demands, to just *be* and listen to God, to their own hearts, and to rest and really connect with those deeper callings, dreams, hurts, joys, and disappointments—a place to be real with themselves and God.

We do this through leading optional times of Lectio Divinia, having resources available, providing meals, and encouraging that electronics be turned off. At one retreat there was a guy that was petrified to do his first solitude retreat. He almost didn't come. As an extrovert, he had never had a weekend alone. He wasn't sure he could do it. This guy ended up not even coming to the optional gatherings, but stayed in full solitude, and by the time the weekend was done, he wanted more solitude! I want this opportunity to be available for many more people! We are planning soon to travel around the nation in a conversion van visiting places that are already leading solitude retreats or that have spaces for quiet (if you know of any places, please let us know!).

Jeremy and I are continuing to pray and look for land to have a retreat space for people one day back in California. We are looking for people to partner with us to create this much needed space for people to get still and listen—to listen to their own voice and listen for God's voice and to just be. I am still seeking to learn along with others how to be a human "being" and not a human "doing."

Practicing Solitude

As I am working on this chapter, I am on day two of a seven-day solitude retreat at a cabin that is on 160 beautiful, spacious acres. This cabin where I am staying is offered for people to "get away with God" and have quiet. It is so peacefully decorated by the hostess, complete with a chocolate on the bed, books to use in solitude, a map that marks the trails, hammocks, places to sit, and a prayer walk. It's the most serene place where one can pray, sing, shout, and cry out loud where no one can hear. I am taking this time during a family crisis where I am responsible for my loved ones' medical care.

One of the books here is by Ruth Haley Barton. In her book *Sacred Rhythms*, she describes the practice of solitude well. I love it in Chapter 2 where she writes that solitude is a place where our soul can safely come out. "There are very few places where the soul is truly safe, where the knowing, the questions, the longings of the soul are welcomed, received and listened to rather than evaluated, judged or beaten out of us." It's a time to enter into "unproductive" being, rather than frenetic doing—a time to be quiet to deeply attend upon your own heart, body and soul—a time to refresh and recenter into what truly matters.

Our pace of life, especially with technology, has left most of us utterly exhausted. Solitude offers a time to shut that down and listen and to be present to God, ourselves and to each other. We are an exhausted people on this earth right now. It's interesting that even Jesus felt the need (along with his disciples) to go away and rest a while (Mark 6:30). Barton also talks about "how important it is to have time and space for being with what's real in life—to celebrate the joys, grieve the losses, shed my tears, sit with the questions, feel my anger, attend to my loneliness." This "being with what is" is not the same as problem solving or fixing, because not everything can be fixed or solved. Rather, it means allowing God to be with me in that place and waiting for Him to do what is needed. In silence my soul waits for God, and God alone.

I find that in these spaces of quieting the outside, I can better understand and hear my own true voice from within. The interesting thing is that I have told retreatants where I have been the leader to expect all manner of things to come against their time to pull away. Guaranteeing them that this will indeed happen before, during, or after their time away, or maybe all three. Of course, with this personal retreat I'm on right now, the first two have already happened.

Getting Quiet on the Inside

I came to a beautiful swing on the opposite side of the property from the cabin, facing the woods and spacious beauty. One of the first things I have noticed on a solitude retreat is how hard it is to get quiet on the inside, to allow the inner chaos to settle so we can hear something! Even though I have worked hard to arrive at this retreat, and I desire to say yes to God's invitations and receive what God has for me, it's not always as easy as it sounds! When external noise has been silenced, we might become aware that the chaos isn't just out there in the world we've left behind, it's also inside of us because of all we bring with us. Most of us have been running so hard and so fast for so long that entering into a retreat feels like coming to a screeching halt after driving much too fast; I found this super interesting because it seems every time I (or most others I know) try to pull away, there are so many roadblocks.

There is also a very real inner noise when it finally gets quiet on the outside. That inner chaos really gets loud! And it's not just the inner noise, it's the constant pull from whatever "emergency" is happening in our lives to come out from the solitude and to take the reins again to fix it. To resist this is *so* hard.

Sometimes I find it takes the first day or two to even begin to get quiet enough to really rest and listen, and even then, it can still be a battle. Right now, I choose to stop, open my hands, listen to the soft chimes, let the sun warm my chilly body, and know that there is a bigger plan. Even in the chaos and unknown, even now, all of a sudden, I do not know where I will live or if I will have a car to drive in two days. I could let this consume my thinking and eat up my entire time left here, whether that is two days or the planned five days. I am not in control and I can rest in that or fight it and be anxious. It will likely be a mixture of both, and that is OK.

You Can't Mess This Up!

The main take away I always share with people on retreats I am leading is that "you can't mess it up." There might not be any big "aha" moments, or big breakthroughs. You may need to just sleep the whole time, walk, journal, cry, or do nothing at all—but you cannot mess it up. I sure needed to tell this to myself today. You have done it right, just by making the decision to leave the chaos of your day-to-day life and pull away. No matter how distracted you are or what happens before, during or after your retreat, it's *all* good. It's all a gift and I can tell even after a day-and-a-half that my soul is quieter within me.

Jer and I long to lead these retreats and other retreats around the nation/world, and to have a spot of land where people can come, pull away, rest, and hear their own true voice from within. We need it regularly ourselves and we know there are many weary people in this world that long for the same thing.

CONCLUSION

I HOPE THAT YOU, dear reader, walk away from this book knowing that your voice is uniquely yours and is so important in this world! Using your voice to tell your unique story can have an impact that you would never believe. If you walk away with anything, I hope it's this: that you recognize that your story, your voice, your struggles and joys all matter deeply—that no matter what you have faced, it's OK to take up space and share your God-given story with your loved ones, a counselor, a spiritual director/ soul companion, or whoever desires to listen.

I hope you have picked up too that I don't have anything "together" or figured out. I am a messy human just seeking to love God and people in any ways that I can. I have had a lot of training. I've had people invest in, help, and believe in me along the way. I also have family and close friends who love me deeply. Yet, even with all of this, I can still feel so deeply lonely sometimes and long for the day to be completely and fully known.

If someone were to tell me earlier in life that I would get

married in my late 30's, not have kids, not be able to do what I thought a "good wife" should do, and that I would be sick for over half of my years lived thus far, I am not sure what I would have done. But the perfect love of God for me has been enough, alongside of experiencing that love in human flesh through Jer's love.

Knowing that God sees and knows all of the mess, my brokenness and failures, yet loves me perfectly, is the reason I can get up in the morning. You are loved, dear one, and accepted as you are. Please listen deeply, find your voice, and speak it! The world will be changed because of it.

Thanks for reading and hanging out with me in these pages. I sure hope to hear from you and hear what you took away from reading this…(if I publish it)!

Coaching Opportunity

If you have found yourself identifying with anything in this book and you want to process any of it with me, then I invite you to reach out. I am a coach and love talking with women about any of the things I shared about in this book. In my coaching, I love using my nursing background, counseling experience, spiritual care, my own experience with illness, coaching experience with others, and every other training and life experience to coach others. Feel free to reach out to me at healthyandwholeforbodyandsoul@gmail.com. You can reach out too even if you have a reflection or question about what I shared in this book. I would love to hear from you!

You can click this QR code to visit my site:

If you found this book helpful, I'd greatly appreciate you sharing it with a friend and leaving a review on Amazon so others can discover their own authentic voice. Thank you from the bottom of my heart! Click the QR code below to order a copy or leave a review on Amazon.

ACKNOWLEDGMENTS

I dedicate this book to the few that have stuck so closely by my side through these recent years—those that were there for me even when I was so sick that I could not reciprocate. I dedicate this book to my family and Jer's family, who we were not able to be in much contact with during the recent years of such struggle, but who I knew loved us and were praying daily for us. I dedicate this to you five dear women who were on the receiving end of my daily texts of cries for help, the voice memos I sent (as I didn't have the bandwidth for live calls), and my updates on the hard—you who gave, loved, listened, started GoFundMes, prayed for hours on end, sent cards and gifts, rallied others to pray, and gathered on Zoom with me to listen to me share and wail out of the pain I was enduring both on a physical and emotional level. You dear five who weekly sent cards without fail, who loved me when I could not love back. You are a huge reason I am still here to write and even to finish this book. I wish the words "thank you" were sufficient, but they are not.

I am so thankful for each of you, individually. I am in tears as I think of missing your long awaited wedding, not being able to see you when you came to visit from out of town and I was too weak to get out of bed, you who were used to having frequent visits on the phone and in person, and you who I had to many times say "no" to about visiting. You who even in your walking out your own hardest of hard, showed up for me anyways. You who I pushed away and felt unworthy of your love, and even got mad and frustrated that you didn't get it or didn't respond in the way I wanted (ugh, my ungrateful, raw, ugly heart at times)—you loved me anyways. You who waited each day for a potential call from Jer saying "she did not make it." You dear sisters have blown me away with your love, and you continue to do so. My world went from feeling so big and abundant with many relationships before March of 2020, to being so very small—to you precious women, and that was more than enough. You ladies have been such safe places for my real, true, authentic, unfiltered voice, even in the most vulnerable times. THANK YOU!

There were so many others too who have loved, written cards, prayed, helped us financially and been faithful encouragers. I am so grateful for every kind act.

My main dedication of this book goes to my one true love. Besides my God, my dear Jer… mi amor...oh love, you have been my rock. The one who has 24/7 seen it all. You have loved me with a love that I did not know was possible. I had always thought that to be a wife I needed to do certain things to earn or deserve this kind of love. But from day one of our marriage, when I pretty much dropped to the ground with Lyme disease, and up until now, I have not *once* had to edit my voice or pretend to be someone I am not. I have never had to earn your love. You have moved us 20 times (pretty much on your own each time because of my illnesses) during our 10-plus years of marriage. You have cooked, cleaned, decorated, worked full time, and been my full-time caregiver (including changing out my IVs and even dressing me when I didn't have the strength to do so). You have listened for sometimes more than five hours at a time (without interrupting even when you had to go to the bathroom!) because that is who you are.

You, my love, have welcomed my rambles and deep heart sharing, listening to my past traumas, and helping me carry my baggage. You have wanted to hear my voice and love me in the worst and *best* of times. Together we have cried until there were no tears left and we have laughed so hard we couldn't breathe. We have made decisions that not one person in our lives understands. You have held me as I wept when we lost our baby. You have literally been by my side through probably 1,000 medical appointments and have kept spreadsheets of sometimes 100-plus symptoms that are all happening at once. You have rushed me to the ER on countless occasions and have kept others updated. You have done all this without complaining even once since I have known you.

You truly are the most realistic picture of Jesus that walks this earth. You are handsome, humble, fun, funny, thoughtful, kind and so so gentle with me. You, mi amor, have been *the one* who has welcomed my true, authentic, unfiltered voice the most, and you have never shut me down—not once. You have shown me that I am loved because I am a beloved daughter of God. I have felt like a failure, as you know, over and over and over. I have not been able to bear children, cook, clean, organize, and so many other things I thought a wife "ought" to do, and you have loved me anyway, and with such joy and delight. I do not get it. I don't deserve you or your love. You have sacrificed everything for me. Now *this* is a picture of the gospel, isn't it? I could not be more delighted that I waited 36 years to marry you, my love, and to you (and to the God who holds us both), I dedicate this book.

STUDY GUIDE
FOR PERSONAL AND SMALL
GROUP REFLECTION

Introduction

1. Heather opens up about feeling hopeless during her bouts with illness. Have there been times when you felt lonely and hopeless? What did you do in those moments?

2. Are there things that you are afraid to share with others out of fear that you'll be rejected?

3. Heather writes about shifting who she was to be liked and approved of by others. What ways, if any, can you relate to this?

4. Do you have an inner critic? What message or messages does your inner critic replay? In what moments does your inner critic show up?

5. What areas of your life do you desire more freedom? How might your life change if you discovered your brave voice?

Chapter 1

1. Heather describes many childhood experiences of not knowing she had a voice. What experiences did you resonate with?

2. What childhood experiences shaped who you are in positive and negative ways?

3. Who were the people in your life who listened to you, who made you feel seen and special?

4. Heather talked about messages she internalized growing up like, "it's not OK to be not OK," or she shouldn't be sad. What are some messages you internalized from family, school, religious communities, or the larger society?

5. Did you ever feel that your acceptance was tied to your performance? How did that make you feel at the time? How does that make you feel now?

6. If you could go back and say one thing to your childhood self, what would it be?

Chapter 2

1. Do you ever compare yourself to other people? What area do you compare yourself the most (physically, financially, vocationally, spiritually, etc)?

2. Have you had times where you felt depressed or struggled with depression? Did you tell anyone? Why or why not?

3. What mentors have you had in your life? What were the most valuable lessons you learned from them?

4. What role has your faith played in helping you either voice your needs or stay silent?

5. Is it easy or hard for you to ask for help? Why?

Chapter 3

1. Have you ever heard the voice of God in yourself? How do you differentiate your inner voice from God's voice?

2. What methods of Bible study are least impactful for you? What methods are most impactful? Have you ever tried Lectio Divina?

3. Heather mentioned wrestling with the "inner dictator." Can you relate to the reality of being harder and more critical of yourself than anyone else?

4. Is it easy or hard for you to hear that you are loved, accepted, forgiven, complete, whole in Christ? What makes it easy and/or hard?

5. Where does your greatest desire and talent meet the world's greatest need?

6. Have you had moments where you followed what your inner voice was telling you over other people's voices? How did it turn out? What did you learn from those experiences?

Chapter 4

1. Do you have trouble saying "no?" Why or why not?

2. Where this week did you have a hard time saying 'no'?" "When did you want to say 'no,' but didn't say it?"

3. Why are "no's" holy?

4. Have you traveled overseas? What places have you been? What places would you like to go?

5. What's the difference between needing people and loving them?

6. As Heather mentioned, fear keeps us from saying "no" to things we don't want and from saying "yes" to things we do want. What are things that you want to say "yes" to but don't because of fear? What are the current "holy yes's" and "holy no's" in your life and what boundaries do you still need to establish to be healthy?

Chapter 5

1. Heather mentions the power of using voice in everyday interactions with people you encounter. Who are some people you interact with on a daily basis? How could you use your voice to make a positive impact in these everyday interactions?

2. How can reclaiming your authentic voice be good for you and the world?

3. What are ways you've kept your word? What are ways you've broken your word? Is there any reconciliation that is needed in any relationships? What is stopping you from reaching out?

4. What are ways you can use your voice to advocate for

others at your job or in your community?

5. Is it easier for you to listen or to speak? Why?

6. What are some ways you can build trust with people who are different from you?

Chapter 6

1. What are situations when it might be better *not* to speak?

2. Where are the places and who are the people where you feel most celebrated and not just tolerated?

3. When have you had the chance to sit at the feet, literally or figuratively, of someone else? What did you learn from that experience?

4. Heather's understanding of immigrants was expanded after hearing their stories. How have her stories of interacting with the houseless and immigrants expanded your understanding?

5. Do you agree that the heart's utmost desire is to be listened to, rather than spoken to? Why or why not?

6. Has fear ever held you back from engaging with different people or cultures? When have you felt the fear, but like Heather, chosen to act anyway?

Chapter 7

1. What is it like for you to read about different examples of domestic violence?

2. Do you know someone(s) in a domestic violence situation? Have you considered offering them resources like Heather describes?

3. Is it hard for you to share your personal struggles with others?

4. Have you ever felt pressure to live up to the unrealistic expectations of someone you were in a relationship with? How did you deal with it?

5. Have you ever been in an unhealthy or destructive relationship? How did you become aware?

6. What are the attributes of a healthy relationship that you have or desire?

Chapter 8

1. Have you ever felt unseen or unheard by medical professionals? What was it like to not have your concerns taken seriously?

2. Have you ever neglected your own needs, voice, or desires to help others?

3. What are ways you can care for yourself while helping others?

4. Heather talks about the importance of listening to your body. Do you listen to your body? What does your body tell you?

5. Is it hard for you to slow down? Why or why not?

6. What was difficult for you about the pandemic? What were some unexpected blessings?

Chapter 9

1. Is it hard for you to use your voice with family? What makes it the most challenging?

2. Can you relate with having to parent your parents? What has that been like for you?

3. If you could tell your family anything, whether they are still alive or not, what would it be?

4. How have your life experiences been like or unlike your parents' experiences?

5. What are some of the unspoken things in your family that have been hard for you? What do you think would happen if you voiced them and talked about them with your

family?

6. What are some things you are grateful for about your family?

Chapter 10

1. What were some times in your life when you really felt you were heard?

2. Who are the people in your life where you can share your unfiltered thoughts and feelings without fear of judgment?

3. What are ways you'd like to cultivate your relationships by listening?

4. Have you ever talked to a counselor, spiritual director, or mentor? If so, what was it like? If not, what do you think it would be like?

5. When's the last time you've offered someone the gift of being listened to? How did the person respond?

Chapter 11

1. Have you ever been on a solitude retreat? If so, how was it? If not, is it something you think you could benefit from?

2. Do you like being alone? Why or why not?

3. When was the last time you were completely alone? What thoughts or feelings did you notice?

4. What are some technologies that distract you from solitude and reflection?

5. How does it make you feel to read Heather say that "you can't mess it up" when it comes to taking time in solitude?

6. Take some time to be still and quiet right now. What is your inner voice telling you?

ADDITIONAL RESOURCES

Book Resources

Ruth Haley Barton, *Sacred Rhythms: Arranging our Lives for Spiritual Transformation* (IVP, 2022)

Barbara Ann Kipfer, *4,000 Questions for Getting to Know Anyone and Everyone* (Random House Reference, 2nd Edition, 2015)

Gabor Mate, *The Myth of Normal: Trauma, Illness, and Healing in a Toxic Culture* (Vermillion, 2022)

Paul Tripp, *Instruments in the Redeemer's Hands: People in Need of Change Helping People in Need of Change* (P&R Publishing, 2002)

Ed Welch, *When People are Big, and God is Small: Overcoming Peer Pressure, Codependency, and the Fear of Man* (P&R Publishing, 2023)

Organizations

Global Immersion – www.globalimmerse.org

Grafted Life Ministries – www.graftedlife.org

Heather's Coaching Business/Ministry –

www.healthyandwholeforbodyandsoul.com

Leslie Vernick & Co – www.leslievernick.com

Organic Intelligence – www.organicintelligence.org

The Simple Way – www.thesimpleway.org